Conte

MW00446910

Tips for entering competitions

Tips for winning competitions

Tools of the trade

Finding your wins

Tips for staying motivated

Introduction

My eyelids felt heavy and I was struggling to stay awake, but I could sense the familiar buzzing of my mobile phone. Frantically grabbing my handbag, I tipped it upside-down and the contents spilled onto the bus floor. "Unknown number" was flashing on the phone and I answered with a sleepy "Hello?" The voice at the other end cheerfully replied "Is that Di?" and I perked up immediately – it was Friday afternoon and there was every possibility this could be a winning telephone call. "It is indeed!" I answered. "Excellent. I'm calling from Electrolux. Do you remember entering a competition with Zanussi last year?"

I certainly did remember. I'd spent ages on my entry and had been daydreaming about getting this phone call. "Well I'm pleased to tell you that from over a thousand entries, we picked your tiebreaker as the winner. You've won a Volkswagen Beetle!"

My jaw dropped. I yelled "I've won a CAR!" at the top of my voice. Everyone on the bus looked round. "I'VE WON A CAR!" I repeated, in shock. I was travelling by National Express bus to Heathrow Airport, about to embark on a three week trip of a lifetime to New Zealand. That too was a prize, my reward for being the first person to solve a Lord of the Rings competition on the Ottakars website.

That moment was when I realised I wasn't just lucky, I was *super* lucky.

I won my first competition prize when I was six. Since then I've dipped in and out of this wonderful hobby, winning over £250,000 of prizes in total. Comping can bring money, magic and excitement to your life. It can give you the means to treat your family and friends to holidays and gifts you could never otherwise afford. And best of all, it costs nothing at all to get started.

Entering competitions and sweepstakes doesn't have to be a time-consuming hobby. Dedicate as little or as much time to it as you like – it's suitable for anyone, from students and mums to full-time workers. But be warned – once you start, you might find it impossible to stop. For many, comping is a hobby that lasts a lifetime, and who can blame them when it offers such astonishing rewards?

In this book you'll find tips for beginners but also plenty of useful advice for those who have been comping for years. This is a fast-moving hobby and none of us know quite where it's going next, so there are always new techniques, apps and websites to discover.

SuperLucky Secrets will help you to win prizes in the way that will be most effective for you. Read it in conjunction with the advice on my blog at **www.superlucky.me** and the tutorials on my YouTube channel at **www.youtube.com/superluckydi**, and you'll discover the type of competition that gives you the best results.

You might be wondering why I want to share my secrets. It's simple. I enjoy helping others to win amazing prizes – I've found something I'm good at, and I want to teach others to be good at it too. Throughout the book you'll hear from lots of winners who have been successful as a result of my tips and advice. What goes around comes around, and I definitely believe in comping karma.

SuperLucky Secrets is presented in sections, starting with the basics and then giving tips on finding, entering and winning competitions. I'll tell you about the tools of the trade, tracking wins, staying motivated, and the things you definitely *shouldn't* be doing. It's not designed to be read in order from start to finish – there's a mixture of tips for beginners and experienced compers, so you may want to skip some of the more advanced tips and move between sections depending on your mood. If you're a brand new comper, have a good read of the **Don't even think about it** section before you start entering any comps.

Remember that comping is a hobby, and the prizes are a bonus. Be patient – some people think they can start comping on Monday and have prizes arriving by Friday! Even if you enter right before a competition closes, the promoter can take weeks to choose a winner, and then they need to organise delivery of the prize, which can take months. A brand new comper will take a while to get in the swing of things, but don't give up if you're not winning. Try something different – there are plenty of ideas in this book that will help you find new ways to win. Stay optimistic and seek inspiration from your new comping friends. I wish you the very best of luck!

Please note, the information in this book is correct at the time of publication. Social networks, websites, software and apps are constantly being updated so the details may change. Technical guidance is generally for iPhone and Mac users using Chrome, so instructions may not be appropriate for all readers. Subscribe to my newsletter at www.superlucky.me/signup and check www.superlucky.me for up-to-date guidance and information.

If you've bought a print copy of 'SuperLucky Secrets', you can also receive an interactive PDF or Kindle version by contacting di@superlucky.me.

The Basics

The tips in this section will ease you into the hobby gently, and hopefully get you excited about what's coming next – finding, entering and winning competitions!

1. Get online

If you want to be successful at comping in the 21st century, simply owning a reporter's notebook and a sheet of second class stamps won't cut it I'm afraid. Modern comping is all about getting online – and not just at home. Ideally you'll have a laptop or tablet (or both!), plus a phone with 3G/4G and a big data allowance so you can enter comps while you're out and about. It's also a worthwhile investment to get a printer, as some prizes are in the form of coupons or codes which you will need to print off and present in-store to redeem your prize.

Smartphones are expensive, but will give you a big advantage in the comping world. You'll have access to email, the internet and hundreds of useful apps, and can enter almost every comp directly from your mobile. If you have a good smartphone, a camera is no longer an essential gadget for photo comps – modern phones take high quality photos and videos, which you can even edit on your phone.

If you're still using a Nokia 'brick' and accessing the internet at your local library, then add a smartphone and laptop to your prize wish list right away – they will make a world of difference to your comping!

2. Write a wish list

Some compers will tell you that success depends on the *quantity* of comps you enter. But most of us don't have the luxury of spending all day long entering hundreds of comps, so it's better to focus on

w/E away, USA, Europe, beds, quality house items, vouchers, money, car, presents, "a year's supply of", my money cant buy experiences eg BAFTA's, 5 star hotels, Macbook *quality,* entering for prizes you really want. Otherwise you'll end up with a garage packed with life-size cardboard cutouts of film stars, football boots signed by an obscure Championship player, or Alaskan salmon cookbooks. Decide what you want to win and make a wish list of prizes – from small things like vouchers and tickets to big things like a holiday or kitchen. If you focus on finding and entering competitions to win those prizes, you'll find the hobby more manageable and enjoyable rather than overwhelming.

When compiling your wish list, try to include a selection of specific smaller prizes – don't fill it with expensive gadgets and holidays. Personally, I love winning tickets to music festivals and gigs, and am regularly the only entrant to local ticket comps in Brighton. Other smaller prizes on my wish list are haircuts, cinema tickets, software and days out to local family attractions. Include gifts for family and friends on your wish list too – I'll never forget my niece's face when I presented her with an iPad Mini this year!

Write your wish list down in a diary, create a collage on your wall, save it in a notes app – or do as I do, and create a board of photos on Pinterest. Searching for those dream prizes is a wonderful way to spend a few hours, and if you've not joined Pinterest yet it's a good way to learn the ropes. Not ready to share your wish list? Then create it as a *secret* Pinterest board for your eyes only. Not sure what Pinterest is? Check out **Pin to win** (tip 53) for how to get started.

Add to your prize wish list all the time, and make sure you refer back to it regularly to keep you motivated and inspired. Looking at your list, take each prize one by one, and think about where you might be able to win it. Search competition listings sites, Google and Twitter regularly to find your dream prizes. Hunt down relevant Facebook pages and follow Twitter accounts – by adding them to **Twitter lists** (tip 24) and **Facebook lists** (tip 22) you can regularly check for comps. Making that wish list is your first step to living the dream!

"Thanks to searching for specific items on my wish list on Twitter, Facebook and Google, I've won three lots of premiere tickets in the past three weeks! I went to Dracula Untold (where my mum got to meet her favourite actor, Luke Evans), The Imitation Game (where I literally brushed shoulders with Benedict Cumberbatch!) and tonight my whole family is going to see Daniel Radcliffe in Horns after we won two pairs of tickets!" – Rachael Simmons

3. Put in the effort

The majority of compers avoid creative or effort comps, but these offer the very best chance of a win and that's why you should get involved. If you only enter simple prize draws, *Retweet & Follow* giveaways or *Like & Share* Facebook promotions, you'll struggle to win much at all – even if you're spending all day long at it. These type of prize draws are easy to enter, which makes them hard to win, because you'll be up against thousands of other compers.

Instead, have a go at tweeting a joke, uploading a photo to Instagram, commenting on a blog, making a purchase, doing a quiz or creating a short video: these competitions are harder to enter, but are much easier to win. In some cases you may well be the only entrant. Don't presume you have to be an amazing photographer or chef – these days you'll find plenty of creative promotions where the winners are drawn at random from all entries, so that disastrous burnt cake could still end up a winner.

Most of the competitions I share at **www.superlucky.me** and the **SuperLucky Facebook page** (www.facebook.com/superlucky. co.uk) involve some element of effort, and I've received some brilliant success stories from my readers – many of whom have been inspired to enter their very first photo competition. You can read about their creative wins in my **SuperLucky Stories** series of blog posts.

"In 2011 I entered my first ever competition with Chevrolet after reading SuperLucky and I won £1,000 cash. Since then, thanks to Di's advice, I've won an iPad Air, Nikon camera and kit, and many smaller prizes worth over £8,000. I am disabled and only enter comps I want to win – this has become my amazing evening hobby" – Caroline Wood

4. Be super social

If you want to be successful at comping, you'll need to get up and running on as many social media channels as you can handle, joining one at a time so it's not too confusing. How many you tackle is up to you, but Facebook and Twitter will give you the most benefits and access to thousands of new competitions. If you like being creative, join Pinterest, Vine, YouTube and Instagram. Even if you don't know what you're doing yet, simply having an account on these networks is enough to get you bonus entries in plenty of prize draws.

As well as social networks, joining a forum is a great way to make comping friends and chat about the latest promotions – see the section on **competition forums** (tip 14) for a selection of the best UK forums to join.

Facebook

Most compers have already joined Facebook – the social network is a wonderful source of competitions, but also a good place to meet like-minded friends. On Facebook you're allowed to have just *one* account, using your real name. You'll certainly encounter compers using nicknames, and running second accounts, but Facebook can shut profile pages down with no warning so it's not worth the risk. It's better to organise your single account by assigning Facebook friends to lists, depending on whether they're close friends, family, compers or workmates. You may see some friends deserting you once you start comping – see tip 9 for how to deal with that. You don't need to add any friends at all if you don't want to – but your account will look suspicious, and you'll find it much harder to find competitions (and your wins!) without a few compers to help. If you join one or two **Facebook groups** (tip 21) you'll find plenty of new comping friends.

Twitter

Twitter is a social network where users send 140-character messages called *tweets*. It's fast-paced and, once you get the hang of it, simple to use – it's also the best way to comp on-the-go as the Twitter app works brilliantly on a smartphone. Companies run prize draws and competitions on the platform because it's a fun way to raise their profile via *viral sharing*. *Retweet to win* giveaways get hundreds of entries, reaching an audience of thousands in the process.

On Twitter you can have as many accounts as you like and there's no need to use your real name. You can have a fun username, but add a real name (forename, surname or both) to your profile. If you already use Twitter for work, introducing competitions to that account is likely to result in your followers dropping like flies. Either warn them that you have a new hobby, or set yourself up a new Twitter account for comping. For more advice on Twitter, see **Make your tweets sweet** (tip 45).

Instagram

Instagram is an app for mobile devices where you take, edit and upload photographs and short videos. You can follow users, like and comment on photos using the website at **www.instagram.com** but can only upload content using the app on your phone or tablet. It's convenient to link your Twitter and Instagram account, and ideally you want to have exactly the same username on each. Even if you don't intend to start using Instagram yet, consider registering your username of choice.

There are lots of competitions on Instagram, some of them with big prizes like cars and holidays, but they can be tricky to find. For how to get started on the app, read **Enter Instagram competitions** (tip 48).

Pinterest

Pinterest is a lovely social network if you're a visual person – it's all about collating 'pins' (images and videos) on themed 'boards'. You can repin things you like from other people's boards, add photos or videos from websites, or upload your own photos and videos to a board. On Pinterest most people use their real name, and link the account to a Facebook profile. For advice on Pinterest comping, see **Pin to win** (tip 53).

Other networks

Snapchat is a relatively new kid on the block, and a handful of companies use it for competitions. Although it's focused on business rather than pleasure, there are a few prizes given away on **LinkedIn**. An advantage of having an account for **Google+** and **YouTube** is getting bonus entries in **Rafflecopter and Gleam giveaways** (tip 52).

5. Always read the rules

It's incredibly important to read the rules – and the T&Cs (terms and conditions) – of a prize promotion, even if you just quickly skim through looking for important dates. It's no good entering a competition that's already closed, or winning tickets to an event you can't attend.

As well as entering them, I run competitions and am amazed at the number of people who don't enter correctly. They comment on a blog instead of tweeting their entry, mis-spell the competition hashtag on Instagram, or even copy the wrong answer from a previous entrant on a Facebook post. Even if you don't have time to read a full set of T&Cs, at least check the entry instructions and make sure your entry is valid. Double check the closing date, as occasionally it will be different on the main website to the T&Cs.

For prize draws and easy comps, you don't need to read T&Cs thoroughly – but for big prizes and any competition you're spending time or money on, it's essential. It's particularly important to check whether the winner is judged or chosen at random, as this should affect the time you dedicate to entering.

Unfortunately, many promoters don't understand the importance of including a closing date in their tweet or Facebook post, and on Twitter there's a lack of any T&Cs at all for most giveaways. Here in the UK, all prize promotions should follow the CAP Code, which states that *"the participant must be able to access the full terms and conditions before they enter the promotion."* Even in a 140-character tweet, promoters should still include a link to the T&Cs. If you can't find them, ask the promoter to send you a link. I spend an awful lot of my time tweeting promoters to ask when the closing date is!

Promoters occasionally choose winners who didn't follow the rules – perhaps they didn't follow the right account on Twitter, or entered using the wrong hashtag. These days, with so many competition entries in the public domain, you can expect a non-valid winning entry to be challenged by a fellow comper. GHD withdrew a prize they awarded to a video entry because a disgruntled entrant (it wasn't me!) pointed out the original tweet clearly said 'submit a *photo*' – in this case, my photo was announced as the new winner.

If you're entering to win a holiday, it's essential you find out what's included and what's not, plus any restrictions on the dates it can be taken. It might be flights only with no accommodation – or accommodation *without* flights. Some prizes can end up costing you rather a lot of money, so make sure you know the details. In some cases a promoter will be flexible if you win a holiday, and arrange for you to take an extra child or two – they may have a certain budget to spend, and can discuss how to spend it with you.

We managed to take Nana with us on our prize trips to Barcelona and the Amalfi coast at no extra cost!

Last year a comper contacted me to say she'd won a trip of a lifetime to America with fixed travel dates – she didn't read the terms, which stated entrants must have a valid passport with six months left on it. She didn't, and had to refuse the prize – don't make the same mistake!

6. Believe you'll win

This is a biggie. These days there are plenty of self-help books about optimism and happiness – and adopting a positive attitude really *can* help you win more prizes. There are lots of compers who say "I don't know why I'm bothering to enter, I'll never win" (unbelievably, sometimes they even waste time typing this as a Facebook comment on a competition!). Comping is about adding a bit of magic to your life – it's about having dreams that really *could* come true. Not on the scale of a Lottery win, of course – but then, the odds of winning a competition are much, much better than the National Lottery jackpot!

Like many successful winners, I believe in the law of attraction – every time I enter a competition I imagine myself with the prize. In some cases I've felt so strongly about winning that I've planned what to say when I get the winning telephone call, or booked time off work for the holiday.

Be confident – when you know you've created an excellent entry for a competition, allow yourself to fantasise about winning. When chatting to friends, don't say "If I win a holiday...", say "When I win a holiday...". People may roll their eyes and laugh, but being lucky comes with hard work and a good attitude – don't stop believing! And if you don't win that particular competition, it's not a failure. To quote famous American comper Helene Hadsell: "There are no failures, only delays in results". Move on, find more competitions and continue to focus on that prize until you eventually win it.

"The biggest prize I've won was £10,000 from Yazoo a few years ago. There was a lot of drama about the weekly voting element, but taking Di's advice I ignored the voting aspect and put all my effort into the main judged prize – and it worked! It was just coming to the end of my undergraduate degree, and I was hoping to carry on to undertake an MA. When people asked me what my post-uni plan was, I didn't want to answer "I'm going to win £10,000 and do a masters", but that was honestly what I was planning to do! It might have seemed mad spending hours constructing a cardboard cop car (which took up the whole living room), but I was convinced I could win. I got the winning phone call the day before my final exam – talk about timing. I've now gone on to be awarded full funding for a PhD, which I wouldn't have been able to do without my Yazoo-funded MA. I'm incredibly grateful. I'm also quite proud of myself for doing something very sensible and not blowing it all on a holiday!" – Laura G

Get organised

You've got the wish list and the positive attitude – now let's get you organised before you really get stuck into comping. This section offers guidance on setting up new emails and profiles, connecting with friends, plus two of my favourite timesavers – lists and bookmarks.

7. Get a new email address

It's worth setting up a brand new email address just for entering competitions, as you'll be getting an awful lot of messages landing in your inbox. Google know their stuff, and I recommend Gmail – sign up for an account at **www.gmail.com**. Try to choose a memorable and short email address, as you will have to write, say, type and spell it thousands of times.

Tips on choosing an email address

- Avoid too many numbers – words are more memorable.

- Don't use underscores or hyphens – they can be easily confused, and are tricky to type in a hurry.

- Don't include your birth year – after all, there are occasions where it's best for a promoter not to know a lady's age (or a gentleman's, actually).

- Avoid any reference to comping or winning – some promoters don't like compers, and *wannawinprizes@gmail.com* might result in a rapid click on the Trash button!

Set up a comping signature

Set up a template or signature in your email software with your full name, postal address, email address and phone number. Set this as the default signature for your comping email, and it will appear at the bottom of each new message you send from that account.

If you need to include an answer, type it at the top of the email before sending. To set your signature in Outlook, click the *E-mail Signature* tab on a message – on a Mac you can create and assign signatures under *Preferences*. Having a saved signature also helps when you need to reply to a WEM (winning e-mail) with your postal address – you'd be amazed how many winners reply with an incorrect house number or postcode because they're so excited about their win!

When you enter a competition via email, always use the specified subject heading – the promoter is likely to be filtering mail according to the subjects. If no subject line is stated, write something relevant, like the name of the publication or prize.

8. Choose a good name and photo

Names, photos and biographies can make all the difference on social media – entrants that appear fun and friendly seem to do rather well. Prize draw winners *should* be chosen at random of course, but you'll notice that smilers do tend to win more prizes. Put yourself in the shoes of the person who's choosing the winner. They are more likely to be scrolling through a list of tiny photos, rather than using a spreadsheet of entries and random number generator. Would they be tempted by a Liverpool FC badge, a blurred dog face or a lady with a big smile? The smile wins (almost) every time – unless it's a comp for a Liverpool shirt!

Your profile photo

Are you still an egg on Twitter, or a silhouette on Facebook? The lack of a proper photo suggests you could be a spamming account – promoters may view you with caution and not fancy the risk of giving you a prize. Make your profile look friendly and real rather than suspiciously sparse. Ideally, upload a photo of yourself rather than your child or pet – if you're shy, be creative! Search the internet for *'create cartoon avatar'* and rustle up a fun profile photo for your social media accounts. I add dozens of members to my comping groups daily and I've seen profile photos of zombie children, hairy bellies and fat cats that are truly horrifying – think about what impression your public profile gives to a promoter.

It's fine to change your profile photo as often as you like: unless you're a 'brand' (for example, a blogger like me) you don't need to worry about consistency across different platforms or websites. Tailoring your photo to appropriate occasions can give you an advantage in competitions: try wearing a Santa hat for the festive season or a moustache for Movember.

Adding a *cover* photo is an option on both Facebook and Twitter – a long group photo of family or friends, or a favourite travel destination will look good.

Username

Use your real name on Facebook – if your name is common, like Sarah Jones, consider adding a middle initial to make it unusual – this helps you when you search for your name on Google too.

On Twitter, don't accept the ugly number-heavy username suggestions they give you when you register. You're more likely to see short, snappy names win prizes – brainstorm combinations of words, for example @BaboonCake or @JulieZing. The kids can be helpful for this! Avoid numbers or underscores – like your email address, your username should be easy to spell, as you'll have to type and write it regularly.

Biography

On Twitter you can add a short biography to your profile. Mention your hobbies – if you're going to be entering for toys and football tickets, you could say you're a mum and a keen supporter of Birmingham City FC. It's up to you whether you mention comping, but it may be best to steer clear. A promoter might pop to your profile page before deciding if you're a winner – so make sure you look like a suitable candidate for a prize! If you're a blogger, include a link to your blog in the biography – influential bloggers often do very well in Twitter giveaways.

9. Connect with comping friends

Comping can be a solitary hobby, and for some people that's the way they prefer it. After all, the busy social side might be seen as an unwanted distraction. But for most of us, the forums, Facebook groups and comp clubs are what make the hobby something really special. Lasting friendships are created, both online and in real life – these new friends will tell you about new promotions, give you advice, post you entry forms and receipts and let you know if they see your name as a winner. Most importantly, they will be there to cheer you up if you're going through a dreaded 'dry spell'.

Facebook friends

The sheer volume of Facebook promotions means that it's swarming with compers, with lots of smaller groups set up to cater for the hobby. It's difficult for new compers to find a welcoming group at first, which is why I set up *'Lucky Learners'* for chat and advice – join us at **www.facebook.com/groups/LuckyLearners**. To find out more about groups and how useful they are for compers, read **Join Facebook Groups** (tip 21).

Your enthusiasm for Facebook giveaways may soon start to grate with your family, workmates and friends, whose news feeds will be full of your Likes and Comments. Unfortunately, you can't stop these activitites from being shown to your friends on their news feed or ticker, so the best option is to message them explaining what *they* need to do about it:

- **Unfollow** – they click the button that says *Following* on your profile page to unfollow you – you'll remain friends but they won't see any of your activity in their news feed.

- **See less posts** – they click on the arrow to the right of your activity in their news feed and choose *Hide post* then *See less from...*

Of course, a few of your friends may be intrigued and fancy getting into the hobby – in which case you should definitely recommend this fabulous comping book you've just bought...

Real life friends

Your next step is to meet a few real life compers – which isn't as scary as it sounds. You could join a local comp club, go to a comping event – or even just meet a local comping friend for coffee. I've met up with compers I've only chatted to on Twitter and Facebook – you don't need to worry about getting along as there will be plenty of competitions to talk about. Sometimes it can be a relief to chat to someone who doesn't think you're completely crazy!

"I have met some wonderful special friends through comping, one in particular who has become like family to me. It's great to share competitions and encourage one another!" – *Carol Burgess*

---

10. Set up comping files

Although people do most of their comping online now, it's still a good idea to use files, boxes or folders to store bits and bobs – for some promotions you're asked to *'keep the receipt safe'* after entering, and may need to post it off to validate a win.

My set-up involves three box files which I keep on a shelf beside my desk:

- **Comps entered** – Using 12 monthly dividers, I file the comps I've entered by the month of their closing date – this might be magazine pages, entry forms, receipts or product wrappers which need to be kept. It's worth keeping competition details in case you win and need to refer back to what the prize is. At the end of December I put the entire file contents into a folder and then I recycle the contents after keeping them for a year.

- **Comps to do** – In this box I put entry forms, promotional stickers, neck collars (from wine or beer bottles), magazine pages and receipts for competitions I've yet to enter. Again, 12 monthly dividers makes this easily manageable – I check the box every week to see I'm up-to-date.

- **Comp club** – This is where I store spare entry forms and magazines for my local comp club meetings.

In my handbag I keep a clear A5 plastic wallet which I use for postcards that need sending, entry forms that need posting in the store, receipts and wrappers I collect whilst out and about. Compers should definitely have a nice sturdy bag, big enough to squirrel away at least 10 free magazines in. Perhaps you could add 'roomy handbag' to your prize wish list?

11. Make the most of your smartphone

Smartphones have made comping an absolute breeze, and if you're yet to upgrade to one, I highly recommend it – make sure you invest in a package with a big data allowance, so you can use 3G or 4G when you don't have WiFi access. There are lots of ways to use a smartphone for comping, and as apps and operating systems get more advanced there will soon be many more. Make sure you know how to copy and paste on a mobile device – watch my YouTube tutorial at **www.superlucky.me/CopyPaste** for tips. Here are a few of my favourite smartphone habits.

Set reminders

Use the calendars and reminders on your phone to remember on-air radio competitions, competition closing dates or Twitter parties. With some phones you can even set a reminder for when you arrive at a certain location – for example, a reminder to pick up promotional apples when you arrive at Tesco. To do this on an iPhone, open the *Reminders* app and tap 'i' next to an item.

Take screenshots

Learning how to take a screenshot on your mobile device is useful, particularly if you use Facebook or Instagram. You can't bookmark from within an app on a phone, so taking a screenshot is an easy way to remember where you spotted a competition – or to capture a winning message! The screenshots will save to your phone's camera roll (or gallery) and you can flick through them to find, bookmark and enter the comps when you have more time. Some competitions actually require you to take a screenshot at a specific point during a video, so this technique is worth learning.

To take a screenshot on an iPhone or iPad, hold down the *Home* button and then press the *Power* button – the screen will flash, you'll hear a click and the photo will be saved to your camera roll. On an Android it's usually the *Power* and *Volume Down* buttons together. With a Samsung Galaxy, you can also take a screenshot by swiping the side of your hand across the screen – this has to be enabled in *Settings > Motions and gestures*, by ticking the *Palm swipe to capture* box. For Windows Phone 8.1, use the Power and Volume Up buttons together – for other devices, search Google to find out which method to use.

Take photos

Get into the habit of using your phone camera for all sorts of things.

- Take photos of promotional codes and barcodes on items like crisp packets, chocolate bars and pop bottles.

- While you're out and about, use your smartphone camera to take photos of competitions on magazine pages, posters, products and in shops.

- Try to build up a good selection of photos on your phone, so if a competition requires a sunglasses selfie, a breakfast photo or a photo of you and your mum, you always have one to hand – see **Take lots of photos** (tip 47) for more advice.

I make the effort to check my camera roll every couple of days to catch up with all the comps I've saved.

Make notes

Most smartphones will have a simple app to use for notes – use this to jot down shopping lists for purchase comps or tiebreaker ideas so you can access and amend it anywhere. I use the **Evernote app** (tip 72) to organise my comping notes, and you can read more about that later on.

Use apps

New mobile apps are constantly being developed, and a few of them are used to host competitions which are generally low entry. There are global apps, national apps for cinema chains, bars or restaurants – and even local apps for your city. When new apps are launched, it's often in conjunction with a promotion.

Three of the most useful apps to download are Shazam, Blippar and Aurasma – promoters link up with these apps to host prize draws on their platforms, and you can read more about these in the **Tools of the trade** section. Apps take up a lot of space on your device, so have a regular clear out of old ones – you can always download them again in the future.

Talk to your phone

Did you know that with some phones, you can speak and your words will be converted into text? It's a brilliant timesaver if you think of a great story or poem and want to quickly remember it, or want to dictate a Facebook comment or tweet. On an iPhone, simply tap the microphone icon next to the space bar on the keyboard – and start talking. You can also ask an iPhone to read texts, emails and notifications to you if you're busy – try holding down the *Home* button, ask Siri to read your emails and he'll read out the senders and subjects to you!

12. Learn to love lists

I love a good list, and technology means my lists can be super efficient. Many compers still like to write traditional lists in their notebook or diary, but for me it simply has to be online lists that synchronise between devices and can be updated when and where I like. Storing lists in *The Cloud*, using a notes app, **Google Drive** (tip 77) or Evernote, is a great idea.

There are lots of ways lists can be used to organise comping, and here are the three I refer to daily:

List of on-pack promotions

A shopping list of on-pack promotions is perfect for when you're out and about. I keep mine in date order, starting with the promotion that ends soonest. You might prefer to keep yours in alphabetical order by product – or even split it into shorter lists for specific supermarkets or shops. I make the product names clickable links to the website, so I can access further information on the promotion if I need to – read more about this in **Evernote** (tip 72).

List of unique codes and barcodes

If you enjoy entering on-pack promotions, you'll know that codes are often printed inside labels, under bottle caps, on messy yogurt lids or butter wrappers. I like to immediately note down the code on my list, so I can throw away or file the wrapper – then I can choose when I want to enter the code online.

List of creative competitions

Most of my big wins come from creative competitions, and that's what I enjoy doing most. I can't bear to miss out on fun comps, so the minute I hear about them, I add them with a closing date to my *to do* list, giving me time to think about my entry.

Like my list of purchase comps, I list creative comps in date order, each one with a clickable link to the terms and conditions. I'll also make notes about any ideas I've had for my entry, and highlight the ones I absolutely *must* enter. When I've entered a comp, I cut it from the list and paste it at the end of the document where I've got an *Awaiting results* section. I go through these links regularly to check that winners have been informed, then delete from my list.

Other handy comping lists you could write are a wish list and a list of prizes you've won – and I bet there are many more!

13. Use browser bookmarks

Browser bookmarks – or favourites – are a great way to organise any kind of web addresses, but are especially useful for compers who visit the same sites and repeat the same searches. Instead of typing in addresses and navigating to the same websites over and over, you *bookmark* them.The Bookmarks (or Favourites) Bar sits underneath the address bar at the top of your browser window for easy access to your favourite sites – simply click an icon to open a website.

You can synchronise bookmarks across your devices – for example, save a bookmark on your iPhone and you'll have it on your laptop too. I've spoken to many compers who waste time using Google search every day to find the instant wins section of my SuperLucky website, when all they need to do is go to **www.superlucky.me/ instantwins**, and add it to their bookmarks bar!

Adding bookmarks varies across browsers and devices, but all should recognise the keyboard shortcut Ctrl+D (PC) or Command+D (Mac). To bookmark using Chrome on a mobile device, tap the three dots in the top corner of the screen and then the star.

Every browser is different when it comes to saving and organising bookmarks, so here are links to specific guidance online:

- Chrome – **http://bit.ly/Chromebookmark**
- Internet Explorer – **http://bit.ly/IEbookmark**
- Safari – **http://bit.ly/SafariBookmark**
- Firefox – **http://bit.ly/FirefoxBookmark**

Using your browser's *Bookmark Manager* you can move and rename bookmarks and add folders – with a mouse you can right-click or Ctrl-click to edit bookmarks quickly. Using folders is a clever way to group lots of sites together, for example daily entry comps, instant win comps, referral comps, local radio stations, and the competition sections of online weekly and monthly magazines.

Bookmark tips

Once you've got the hang of using bookmarks, there are several ways you can use them more efficiently.

- Create folders for specific **Google searches**, **Facebook groups**, **Facebook lists**, **Twitter lists** and more.

- Set up a *Comps to do* folder and bookmark on-the-go from your smartphone – when you have more time open the folder, go to each bookmark, enter the comp, then delete the bookmark.

- Right-click/Ctrl-click on a bookmarks folder with a mouse and you'll get a drop down menu offering the option to *Open all bookmarks* in that folder, so you can rattle through daily comps quickly. Right-clicking also allows you to edit/delete individual bookmarks and folders.

- Save space and squeeze more into your Bookmarks bar by shortening names – if the site has a recognisable favicon (small picture), edit and remove the name entirely.

It may take you a while to set up and organise your comping bookmarks – but once you get the hang of using these shortcuts, it will give you *hours* of extra comping time. You'll find more clever ideas for bookmarks as you read through the book – and I'm sure you'll come up with some of your own too.

Tips for finding competitions

This section will introduce several ways you can find competitions, ranging from the easy (listings websites) to the ingenious (monitoring other compers). You'll learn about Advanced Google searches, Twitter lists and much more!

14. Visit competition listings sites and forums

Most new compers will start by stumbling across big competition websites as a result of an internet search, and it's a great introduction to the hobby. These sites list competitions from here, there and everywhere and you'll quickly become aware of the sheer volume of prize promotions that are out there. Listings websites and forums make it easy for you to find and enter competitions, and some even offer a *tracker* service to remember what you've entered.

Listings sites

The main listings site in the UK is **www.theprizefinder.com**. All the competitions listed are genuine, but watch out for affiliate links to data collection websites such as My Offers, as your details will be sold on to various companies (loans, gas and electric suppliers, insurance companies etc.) and generate lots of spam email. Check the terms and conditions before you enter, and avoid ticking boxes to accept further information from other companies.

Comping forums

If you want to be certain you're not clicking on spam-generating adverts and links, you could stick to entering competitions posted on forums by the members. It's rare for a spam or scam promotion to feature, as they are usually quickly flagged up and removed by the admin team. Examples of free UK comping forums are **MoneySavingExpert**, **Loquax** and **HotUKDeals**.

MSE is the most extensive and useful, but can be tricky for new compers to navigate, so read the help posts and guidance before getting involved. The Loquax forum is very well organised, with icons and sections to help you focus on the type of competition or prize you prefer.

You can access my up-to-date list of UK competition sites with advice on the ones you should avoid at **www.superlucky.me/ CompetitionWebsites**, and you'll find a few worldwide sites listed in the **Resources** section at the end of the book.

15. Get out and about

Sitting at home with a laptop is certainly the easiest option for compers, but getting out and about on a competition hunt gives you an advantage over the thousands that only enter comps they find online.

You'll be surprised where you find competitions – and if you have a smartphone you can enter most of them there and then. Shops, restaurants, cinemas and bars often have entry forms or promotions advertised on posters or flyers. Don't be embarrassed about going into a shop and asking about a competition you've heard about – I'm regularly asking the manager to go 'out back' and have a look for entry forms or POS (point-of-sale) materials like posters and shelf labels!

Supermarkets are full of prize promotions – check the newspapers and magazines for comps, then walk down every aisle looking for 'WIN!' on products and signs. Look at stickers on packaging and neck collars on wine – double check the closing dates as sometimes the staff leave promotional stock on the shelves for months.

Always enter 'one winner per store' promotions if you spot them – Wilkinson and Asda sometimes run these. This type of promotion usually involves a purchase; you have to send off a receipt with an entry form, clearly stating which store you're entering for. Clever compers won't just enter for their nearest store – they will enter for family members at *their* nearest stores too. You can easily pick up several prizes in the same competition if your family are widespread.

Shopping centres and designer outlets regularly give away vouchers to spend there. As well as following them on social media, look out for promotions advertised in the centre itself. Last year I bagged £500 to spend at Bridgend Designer Outlet (in a Pinterest comp with just 2 valid entries) and £250 to spend at Brighton Churchill Square (I was the *only* valid entrant). Westfield and Intu have some fun and generous promotions in their UK shopping centres.

16. Read magazines, newspapers and comics

When I first started comping in the 1990s, all my big wins came from postal competitions in magazines and newspapers. It's different now of course, and the majority of comps are online – but that means a great chance of winning a competition if it *only* features in a printed publication. It's still possible to find a few magazine comps, especially locally. A good tip is to spend time leisurely browsing in a local bookstore or WHSmith – this is a great way to pass time at the airport. Flick through magazines, discreetly taking photos of any email or postal entry competitions, then buy a couple which feature an entry form. You *could* leave without buying anything of course, but the shop might not welcome you back!

Kids' comics

If you have children, comics and magazines are brilliant for winning toys. Look for the ones which have an entry form printed inside and *no* email option, so the only entries will come from people who have purchased the comic. My favourite UK boys' comics with entry forms are Kick and Toxic, but there are new ones in the shops all the time. Unfortunately they're usually in plastic wrap so you can't flick through, but most of them have the same competition format for each issue so you should know what to expect. Always keep an eye out for new kids' comics, or very specialist character comics that only last a few issues. Get an entry in for the early issue prize draws and you won't have much competition – I won £200 of toys from a postcard draw in issue number 2 of the Playmobil comic. Read more tips in **Enter Kids' Competitions** (tip 62).

Magazines

There aren't many entry form draws in mags now, but you might spot email comps hidden away in the editorial. Write in to letters pages and send daft photos off to weekly women's mags. It's worth looking for specialist magazines if you have a hobby like fitness, cycling, camping, fishing or golf – they don't get many submissions for the letters page. Local free magazines are a great source of comps, you can find them in shops, hair salons, bars, libraries and restaurants. Keep an eye out for photo competitions that ask you to feature a magazine too – if you're off to a far-flung destination it may be worth buying the magazine to take along.

Puzzle magazines and weeklies

There are nice cash prizes in UK puzzle mags and women's weeklies, but if you don't have the time or inclination to complete the puzzles yourself, you can always check forums such as Money Saving Expert. Generous forum members post the answers online for others to copy – remember it's polite to thank the poster!

Newspapers

Your local newspaper is a good source of competitions – there's usually a free entry route (email or online), so choose that instead of a pricey text message or phone call. If it's a prize you really fancy, you could splash out on a stamp and create a homemade postal entry – I can confirm that this method still works for local comps!

National newspapers feature short-lived competitions – the free UK paper *Metro* occasionally prints keywords which have to be texted in the same day. This type of competition often doesn't make it onto the online comping forums, so will be low entry. Newspapers regularly give cash prizes to letters and top tips so keep a look out for those too.

17. Listen to the radio

Radio stations are a good source of prizes – and not just on-air competitions, which are much less common since the controversies of the 2000s, where some UK radio stations admitted they faked winners! In the UK, listen to national stations Heart, Magic, Kiss, XFM and Absolute for the biggest prizes. Tune in on a Monday morning to find out which competitions are coming up that week, or a Friday to hear about any weekend promotions. Breakfast and drive-time shows are the most popular for phone or text-in comps.

The websites of your favourite local stations sometimes have exclusive competitions too. You might find entry forms to pre-register for an online comp, perhaps telling a story or completing a tiebreaker sentence. These offer a good chance of a win, as the station will be calling *you* rather than you waiting for the the on-air prompt to call in. I've pre-recorded a competition on Sunday evening, which was broadcast 'as live' the following morning. The comp hadn't even been promoted on air – I found it online and was the only person who had signed up, so it's worth checking the main terms and conditions page just in case you get a preview of what's coming up.

Follow local stations on Twitter and Facebook for the latest competition news. If you have friends locally, you could each listen to a different station and share details of promotions in a secret Facebook group.

"Working together as a small group we would research which radio stations had regular competitions, the times and telephone numbers. I personally won trips to Hong Kong and Austria, along with spa breaks, cash and gadgets!" – Julie Ellis

18. Improve your Google search technique

Searching Google is a great way to find new competitions, particularly if you're looking for specific prizes or local promotions. Or you might simply be searching for new comps to share on a forum!

It's not enough to type "win a holiday" though – there are adjustments which will make your Google searches efficient and relevant, the most important being the location and time settings.

Conducting a successful search

- Go to **www.google.com** (log in if you have a Google account) and type *win* and your desired prize, eg. *win Italy holiday*, in the search box and hit **Return**.

- When you get the results, click **Search Tools** on the bar above the results (on a mobile device you may need to tap the **More** menu to find this option) to get a new set of options underneath.

- Change **Any Country** to your country of choice and change **Any Time** to a date range of your choice – I like to use **Past Week**.

Tips on filtering search results

- If you want to exclude words from your search results, simply add a dash (minus sign) before the word eg. *win holiday*

-Australia would give you holiday competitions but NOT any web pages that mention Australia.

- When you put a phrase in quotes, the results will only include pages with the same words in exactly the same order as what's inside the quotes – for example *"win a family holiday"*

- Type OR in capital letters to search for pages that may have just one of several words, eg. *Win competition Spain OR Italy holiday* gives results for both destinations – without the OR, Google would only show websites that match both Spain and Italy.

- If you want to restrict your search to a certain website, use *site:* before the site address, removing any www or http://, eg. *win Macbook site:forums.moneysavingexpert.com* will only show you results from the MSE forum. Try this for *site:facebook. com* or *site:instagram.com* too!

- If you want to exclude certain websites from your search, simply add a dash (minus sign) before site: eg. *-site:myoffers. co.uk* would exclude comps listed on the My Offers website.

- Try experimenting – you can combine different filters or terms in your search box, eg. *Spain OR Italy "win a family holiday" -site:topfox.co.uk -site:myoffers.co.uk*

- Search for wishlist prizes, favourite competition types and local competitions – also think about phrases that you might find in T&Cs such as *judged on creativity, words or less, closing date for entries* – all these should give you results that are prize draws or competitions.

- Love Rafflecopter or Gleam? Try doing a search restricted to the past few days using the phrases *"a rafflecopter giveaway"* or *"Gleam widget"* to find new giveaways.

- Use **browser bookmarks** (tip 13) to save your searches so you can check them regularly for the latest competitions.

- Your search results might show annoying ads from survey sites like My Offers – if they do, click on the small down arrow next to the website name, go to *Ads Settings* and block the advertiser.

- There's advice on filtering search results using different devices on **Google Support forums**.

If you'd like more help with your Googling, watch my six-minute video guide to searching at **www.superlucky.me/GoogleSearch**, then have a go at setting up some searches for your own most wanted prizes. I use Google searches to look for gig and festival tickets with great success!

Google Alerts

When you're happy with your search terms, you can also use them to set up Google *Alerts*, where you will receive emails when Google finds new search results. To set up an alert, go to **www.google.com/alerts**.

- In the *Create an alert about* box, enter your search terms, using the same format as your regular Google searches.

- Click *Show options* to choose how often you get alerts, what types of results you want to get, and more.

- Click *Create Alert*.

19. Visit company websites

All of us have brands, products and companies that we love, or restaurants and shops that we always visit, so it makes sense to search for prizes related to these. For example, I love Dermalogica skincare, Vans shoes and Yo! Sushi – so am always looking for comps to win these products, or at least vouchers to buy them!

Use your prize wish list as a basis for your search, think of the brands, manufacturers, places and products related to each prize on your wishlist. For example, if you want a coffee machine try

Alerts for wins

FAT FACE
WHITE STUFF
MANTARAY
JOHN LEWIS
WAITROSE
AMAZON

DeLonghi, Morphy Richards, Prestige, Krups, Percol, Nescafé, Kenco, etc.

Search Google for the promoters' websites, and register to join their mailing lists with your comping email address. Then look for links to their social media pages (usually in icon form at the foot of the web page), and click through to each one:

- **Blog** – *Subscribe* via email (see tip 20).

- **Twitter** – *Follow*, and perhaps tap the gear icon to *turn on notifications.*

- **Facebook** – *Like* the page, and perhaps add to an Interest list or Get Notifications of every post they make (do this by clicking *Liked*, then choosing *Get Notifications*).

- **Pinterest** – *Follow all* boards.

- **Instagram** – *Follow* their account, and perhaps set notifications (tap the three dot menu and *turn on post notifications*).

The promoter might also have a YouTube channel, Google+ page or even a mobile app – check all these for giveaways. This is a fun way of searching for competitions – the less well-known the brands and companies are, the more chance you'll have of finding a low entry competition, especially with local companies.

20. Follow blogs

First of all, what is a blog? The word is an abbreviation of *web log*, and it's an online journal of individual posts, displayed in reverse chronological order, with the most recent first. Blogs are designed to be interactive, with readers leaving comments, so can be seen as a type of social network. Most *bloggers* will publish several posts a week, and lots of companies have blogs where they post the latest news. A few of us even blog about comping! Blogs are a great source of low entry prize promotions, because you usually have to leave a comment or log in to a **Gleam or Rafflecopter** giveaway 'widget' to enter – this puts off many prospective entrants.

There are several ways you can keep up to date with your favourite blogs:

Use Bloglovin'

Sign up for Bloglovin' at **www.bloglovin.com** and search for the blogs you like – or simply click on the *follow me on Bloglovin'* badge on the blog itself. Bloglovin' is most useful when you install the mobile app, and gives you an easy scrollable feed of the latest posts from the blogs you follow. You can follow my SuperLucky blog at **www.bloglovin.com/superluckydi**.

Follow on Facebook

You could *Like* the Facebook pages of the blogs you enjoy, as bloggers always share their new posts and giveaways on Facebook. Unfortunately you don't see many page updates in your Facebook news feed, so instead you could add the pages to a new *'Blogs'* **interest list**.

Subscribe by email

Signing up for email updates whenever there's a new post on the blog is the best way to ensure you're first to hear the news, and some blogs might send out a weekly or fortnightly newsletter. To subscribe, pop your email into the box that should feature on the blog's side bar – you may have to click a confirmation email to ensure you're added to the list.

For a selection of great blogs to follow, check out my monthly SuperLucky 'linky' lists, which list hundreds of current giveaways – find them at **www.superlucky.me/linky**. You could also try searching Google or Twitter for the word 'giveaway' along with words related to the type of prize you want to win: travel, beauty, baby, kids etc.

21. Join Facebook groups

Facebook is full of keen compers, and as a result there are hundreds of groups set up to share information and advice. Groups can either be *Public*, *Closed* or *Secret* and sizes range from two members up to 10,000!

- **Public groups** are visible on search results, and you can see all the posts without joining. You'll have to join – and be approved by an Admin – to like, comment or post in a public group.

- **Closed groups** are visible on search results, but you can only see the *About* section and member list. You'll have to join – and be approved by an Admin – to see the posts.

- **Secret groups** aren't visible on search results, so you can only join if an existing member invites you. The link can't be shared with a non-member.

If you're new to Facebook, you might find your request to join a group ignored – just in case, make sure your profile is set to public and that you have a few visible competitions on there.

I run a handful of Facebook groups which you're welcome to join. You'll be approved more quickly if you message me at **www.facebook.com/dicoke** mentioning this book!

- **Lucky Learners** is a closed group for compers worldwide, designed to help and support new recruits to the hobby. Join the group at **www.facebook.com/groups/luckylearners**.

- **Competition Winners** is a public group for sharing UK Facebook winners lists, so winners can search for their name and tag other winners. Join the group at **www.facebook.com/groups/CompWinners**.

- **Facebook Competitions** is a closed group for sharing UK Facebook prize draws and competitions. Join at **www.facebook.com/groups/LuckyLearnersComps/** – you'll have to be a member of the Lucky Learners first.

- I've also compiled a list of local Facebook comping groups in the UK at **www.superlucky.me/FBgroups**, which is updated regularly as people set up new groups.

As you become more confident you might want to search for, join, or even set up:

- your own local competition group.

- a specialised group focusing on a type of competition, eg. Pinterest, photo, kids, radio or blog giveaways.

- a group to swap prizes with other compers.

If you join a Facebook group for sharing competitions you'll be expected to share as well as take information – and do check the *About* section and any group rules before posting. A small friendly Facebook group can be an excellent source of low entry competitions.

If you use Facebook groups regularly, add to your **Favourites menu** by going to **www.facebook.com/groups/?category=membership** and clicking *Add to Favourites*. You'll then be able to access them quickly from the left hand menu (on a computer) or the top of the *More* menu on a mobile device. Alternatively, downloading the free Groups app at **www.facebookgroups.com** shows all your groups in one place.

Notifications from groups can be rather overwhelming – to adjust the amount you get (or turn them off completely) click *Notifications* on the group's cover photo. On a mobile device, tap *More > View Group Info > Edit Notification Settings*.

22. Use Facebook lists

Facebook lists are a convenient way to organise your friends and the pages you like – and a great way to find competitions. There are two types of list to create on Facebook. *Interest lists* feature Facebook pages and people, and *Friends lists* feature just your friends.

Interest lists

If there are certain types of prizes you're after, you'll love interest lists. Facebook page updates are only sent to a tiny percentage of fans, so adding pages to an interest list gives you a better chance of seeing relevant content – my own lists include home and garden pages, holiday companies and local Brighton pages. As well as setting up your own lists you can *Subscribe* to an interest list that someone else has created.

Creating an interest list

Go to **www.facebook.com/bookmarks/interests** (or click *More* next to *Interests* on the left hand menu) then:

- Click *Add Interests*, then *Create List*.
- Search for the people or pages you want to add to your list using the search box at the top of the page – you don't have to like a page or follow a person to add them to a list, and people won't know that they've been added.
- Click *Next*, and choose a name for the list.
- Select a privacy setting – choose *Public* if you want others to be able to subscribe to your list, or *Private* so it's only visible to you. Private is best, so people can't copy your hard work!
- Click *Done*.

Adding to an interest list

- You can add a page to an interest list from the page if you're already a fan – click *Liked* and then *Add to interest list*.
- After adding to a list, you can also choose to *Unlike* the page – it will remain on your list.

A few suggestions for interest lists

- Favourite comping pages and compers, for a regular feed of the latest comps.

- Local restaurants, shops, beauty salons, magazines, garden centres, newspapers etc.

- Favourite restaurant or pub chains, plus the grocery products you use most at home.

Friends lists

Friends lists are a great way to organise your friends – for example, you can share comping related posts with a *Compers* list, and share family photos to your *Close Friends* list. A friend can feature in as many lists as you like.

Creating a friends list

- Go to **www.facebook.com/bookmarks/lists** (or click *More* next to Friends on your left hand menu).

- Click *Create List*.

- Name your list (eg. *Compers*) then type in friends names to add them and click *Create*.

Adding to a friends list

There are a few ways you can add your friends to a list – you should get into the habit of assigning new friends to lists as soon as you accept or add them.

- At the top of a friend's profile page, click on *Friends > Add to another list*. On a mobile device, tap *Friends > Edit Friends Lists*.

- You can add to a list when you confirm a friend request – after clicking *Confirm*, wait for it to show the *Friends* button then click it and choose *Add to another list* (this won't work on a mobile device, you will have to go to their profile page after adding, and tap *Friends* to add them to a list)

- When you send a request, click *Add Friend* – wait for a moment, then click on *Friend Request Sent > Add to another list*.

Viewing a list

- On a computer, look for *Interests* on the left hand menu of your home page, hover over it and click *More* to see all your lists.

- Click the settings (gear icon) and you can add a list to your *Favourites*.

- Click on the list name to view a news feed from that list – you might want to bookmark this feed to make it easy to find.

- On a mobile device, find your lists by tapping *More* (three lines) then scrolling down to *Feeds* – tap it to show all your lists, then tap a list name.

When you view a list, you're actually seeing a *news feed* from that list – activity from the list members. A news feed from compers not only shows you the posts the members are sharing, but also which pages they are liking – and if a comper likes a page you can be 95% certain there's some type of giveaway on it!

If you want to enter a Like, Comment or Share competition that features on a list feed, you'll have to click the photo to go to the original post on the promoter's page. For advice on how to enter Facebook comps, see the **Have fun with Facebook** section (tip 40).

23. Search Twitter

Don't skip this tip if you aren't registered with Twitter and don't tweet – you can still use Twitter's excellent search to find competitions hosted on websites, Facebook, Instagram, Pinterest and more. Twitter is used by most local and national businesses to share their current promotions, and is a valuable resource for compers.

How to do a simple Twitter search

- Go to **www.twitter.com/search** or tap the magnifying glass icon on the mobile app. Type in words or hashtags – eg. *'win holiday'* and hit Return to search. Play around with different word combinations: *'win competition'* will give you lots of results, but search for *'reply with win'* and you'll narrow your search to Twitter comps that require a reply.

- When you get the results, click to change them from *Top* to *Live* (or *All*, if you're using the app) – the default *Top* results will show you older, more popular tweets but *Live (or All)* will show you the most recent results.

- You'll probably end up with a real mish-mash of results; some will be Twitter giveaways but there will also be links to competitions – and probably some completely unrelated tweets too. Scroll through and if you spot anything good, enter it there and then, or tap the star to add to your Favourites.

- Depending on your search terms, clicking *Photos* may also give you a selection of competitions. On the mobile app, when you have your search results, tap the slider icon in the right of the search box and choose *Photos* – view as a list or grid view, where you can click a photo to see the attached tweet.

How to do an advanced Twitter search

You can create a more detailed search at **www.twitter.com/search-advanced**. Specify hashtags, dates, tweet types, or even restrict your search near a certain location.

If you enjoy searching Twitter for comps, download the **Tweetdeck** app (tip 144) to your computer, which allows you to run several searches simultaneously.

For advice on entering Twitter comps, see **Make your tweets sweet** in the next section and visit **www.superlucky.me/twitterguide**.

"I never used to win anything on Twitter through the usual 'RT & Win' comps but when I started searching for specific prizes and changing the filter to "Live Tweets" it opened up so many smaller, less obvious Twitter comps. Since then I've won tons!" – Rachael Simmons

24. Use Twitter lists

If you register with Twitter and enjoy using it, getting to grips with lists will help your comping.

Create lists and add any user to them – you can also be added to a list yourself. Subscribe to other people's lists by visiting their profile page, clicking *Lists* and then *Subscribe*. To view a list, go to a profile page, tap the settings (gear) icon and choose *Lists*, then *Subscribed to* or *Member of*. Tap the list name and you can opt to view the tweets, list members or subscribers.

Creating lists

*   If you're using the Twitter website, click your profile photo and choose *Lists* from the drop-down menu – on a mobile device, tap on the settings (gear) icon near your photo and tap *Lists*.

*   Choose *Create New List* (desktop) or tap the plus sign (mobile)

*   Name your list and choose *Public* or *Private* – anyone can see and subscribe to a public list, for comping purposes I recommend you create all lists as private.

*   To add to a list, go to a user's profile page, tap the settings (gear) icon and choose *Add/Remove from lists...* then select the list to add them to.

Using a compers list

It's good manners to follow your comping friends, but with the Twitter follow limit set to 2,001 accounts (until you reach a certain number of followers yourself), you'll soon be struggling to follow promoters. Adding comping friends to a list rather than following them offers several benefits:

*   It frees up space for you to follow other accounts.

*   A compers list is a handy source of competitions – add the link to your Bookmarks Bar.

- Your main newsfeed will become more manageable, not just a list of compers' retweets.

If you've been added to a public list and want to be removed, the only way to do this is to go to the list creator's profile, click *Block* and then *Unblock*. That will remove you from their list. Unfortunately, you can't find out which private lists you've been added to.

Adding promoters to lists

You might decide to create Twitter lists for promoters – perhaps companies that always run a #FreebieFriday competition, or maybe local companies who run giveaways, or your favourite toy companies if you're winning prizes for Christmas.

Lists are a great way for you to focus your comping and find competitions – have a play and see what you come up with. You might find my video guide at **www.superlucky.me/EnterTwitterComps** useful when setting up your lists - start viewing at around 12 minutes 30 seconds.

25. Search for hashtags

A hashtag is a word or phrase beginning with a hash sign (#), used most commonly on social media to identify comments, posts or tweets on a specific topic. Hashtags aren't case sensitive, and can't include spaces – so you'll sometimes have to spend time working out what the hashtag is.

Promoters might use hashtags for certain competitions or prize draws to track entries or as a promotional tool – for example Dreams Beds conjured up the #Yawnie hashtag last year. Others use their name as part of the hashtag to ensure it's unique to them, eg. #RustoleumMakeover. If you spot a hashtag on Facebook, Twitter or Instagram then click or tap it to show all the tweets, posts or photos with the same hashtag. It's a quick way to check out the entries you're up against in a photo or tiebreaker comp.

There are a number of generic hashtags you can use to find competitions online.

- *#competition, #comp* (UK/Australia/South Africa)
- *#sweepstakes, #sweeps, #contest* (US/Canada)
- *#giveaway* – often used for blog giveaways
- *#win* – rather generic, but worth a try!

On Instagram you can only search on a single hashtag – in the UK, #competition is your best bet. Scroll through the photo results quickly looking for anything with text on that suggests a prize promotion. In 2015 Instagram made hashtags clickable on the Instagram website, for example you can conduct a search on #competition at **http://instagram.com/explore/tags/competition**

On Twitter you can search for any number of hashtags together, eg. *#Competition #MothersDay* – check your **Comping Calendar** (tip 65) as there are plenty of occasions where searching for #win along with a specific hashtag will give good results.

General hashtags like #giveaway aren't very effective on Pinterest or Facebook, as the results aren't in date order – you may have better luck combining it with a specific event hashtag, eg. #WorldBookDay #win.

One Saturday morning while waiting for the kettle to boil I had a browse on Twitter and spotted it was World Gin Day. I searched for the #WorldGinDay hashtag with the word Win and found several comps to enter – one of them only had four entries, and I was delighted to win a £45 bottle of Firkin Gin!

26. Copy successful compers

The big advantage – and disadvantage – of modern comping is that almost *everything* is public. Compers can't expect to enter a competition on social media and keep it a secret! On the other hand, seeing what other compers are up to is a resourceful way of finding new competitions. Find successful compers by looking to see who's picking up all the prizes, especially in creative competitions. Add them to Facebook and Twitter lists, get notifications of their social media posts, or bookmark links to their social profiles.

If you're going to *stalk* compers, do it discreetly. Bookmarking is the easiest and least intrusive way of seeing what they are up to – create a new bookmarks folder and fill it with Instagram profiles, Twitter feeds and Pinterest profiles, then check it regularly.

There are plenty of other ways to keep tabs on successful compers.

Twitter

- *Follow* their comping account, click settings (gear icon) and choose to *Turn on notifications*. If you don't want to follow them, add them to a private **Twitter list** (tip 24) or simply bookmark their profile page.

- When they tweet a competition entry, check to see if they're replying to a tweet where you can find details of the comp.

- If they're a creative comper, click on *Photos & Videos* to see what media they've been tweeting, then click the hashtag to find the original competition post.

- From their profile page, click *Favourites* to see which tweets they've been starring. Test this out with *@SuperluckyDi*, as I'm always favouriting competition tweets to check out later when I have more time.

Facebook

- If you've added lots of comping friends, Facebook's *ticker* is an excellent way to find competitions. Essentially it's a live feed of everything your friends are up to *right now*. Add lots of busy compers as friends, and start clicking. You can find the ticker on the right of your browser window – it only appears on a desktop PC or laptop, and you may need to drag to widen your window. If you don't have it, click the settings (gear icon) and choose *Show ticker* – unfortunately not everyone has this option. If you have comping friends, you'll see plenty of action and comps on your ticker – hover over the news stories to expand them.

- On Facebook you can choose to receive a notification every time a friend posts an update – simply click *Friends* and then *Get Notifications*. This isn't possible using the mobile app, you'll have to use a browser and *view desktop site*.

- Add friends to a **compers list** on Facebook.

Pinterest

- In your settings menu, go into *Account settings* to set email or push notifications. Pinterest notifies me on my phone every time someone I follow adds a new board – these are often competition entries, so I open up the app to find out what competition the board is for.

Instagram

- On Instagram you can be notified each time someone you follow posts a photo: simply tap the menu icon (three dots) on their profile and choose *Get post notifications*.

- If you spot entries on a comper's profile, look for tagged promoters and competition hashtags in the captions – click these and scroll until you track down the competition post with the details.

You might find it strange to 'stalk' at first, but lots of people do it (I certainly have a few stalkers!). If you're concerned about people stalking your own timelines, follow my advice on **keeping a secret** (tip 58) – and make sure you enter competitions at the last minute!

27. Plan your day

If you're heading somewhere, look for specific promotions in advance of your journey. Search on Google and Twitter, check Facebook pages of shopping centres you're heading to and look in the local newspaper or events guide. Dining out? Check restaurant chains like *Pizza Express, Zizzi, Frankie & Bennys, Yo! Sushi, Wagamama, Bella Italia* and *Prezzo* – all these have had recent selfie competitions.

Comping in London

A day trip to London is great fun for compers. Check on the *Selfridges, Harrods, Liberty* and *Harvey Nichols* Facebook pages to see if they have current promotions. *Carnaby Street, Regent Street* and *Oxford Street* do regular Instagram, Facebook and Twitter promotions.

Search for *spot taxi win* on Twitter – it's a classic promotion to photograph a taxi advertising a certain brand. Last summer I was early for my train at St. Pancras so watched the taxis line up at the rank – I snapped a photo of a Celebrity Cruises cab and won a fabulous VIP day out at the polo!

You can also search for *'win tube poster'* or *'billboard London win'* – I won a TV after taking a selfie in front of a poster at a tube station. Feeling generous? Take a few extra photos of taxis, posters or shop windows for your friends to tweet too.

The UK free daily newspaper Metro runs a lot of competitions, and a couple of years ago they gave away an iPad every day for a week. To enter, you had to take a photo of the Metro advert showing on the large screens in London train stations. On a night out I took my husband, Rob, on a detour to London Bridge station, where we waited for 15 minutes for the ad to appear. We both tweeted a photo – and the following day he got a winning tweet! This hard-to-enter photo and location specific competition got less than ten entries each day – it was worth the effort.

Launch events

When a new store opens there's likely to be a promotion to celebrate. Quite often you'll hear advertising on your local radio station letting you know when the opening day is. Sometimes the first 100 people will get a goody bag, a discount and entry into a prize draw.

When the Nottingham branch of M&S opened their new electrical department, there was an ad in the local paper promoting an instore prize draw to win an HDTV. I popped in on my lunch break but the two members of staff knew nothing about it – even when I showed them the advert. A true comper doesn't give up easily though, so I called a member of the management team over – he knew what it was, and rummaged under the counter, eventually producing a big 'post your entries here' box, along with a stack of blank entry forms. Mine was the first entry in the box, and I won!

"Comping has given me and my entire family some amazing experiences. Some of them have been prizes such as a holiday to Turkey, a family trip to Lapland, several weekends away including Paris, the Lake District, a boutique break in Brighton and my biggest win to date – £15,000 from Loose Women, which we used to build a garden room at the back of our house. But some have just been what we've had to do to enter a competition, such as searching round London for the Tumi golden luggage or finding the Johnson tiled wall in Clerkenwell. Comping even makes going shopping an interesting experience as I'm always looking out for new competitions or qualifiers for those I already know about." – Andrea Goodheart

---

28. Go to shows

What kinds of shows? All kinds of shows! Consumer shows, trade shows, country shows, local craft shows, baby shows... all shows have some form of prizes on offer. Check venue websites like Birmingham NEC or London Excel to see what shows are coming up and do a Twitter or Google search on *win tickets* with the event name. You should *never* have to pay to go to a major show – free tickets and competition prizes are everywhere. Don't miss out on trade shows too – the public are usually welcome. When you're going to a show, check what other shows are on at the same time and look for free tickets to those too.

At the show, be confident and friendly rather than just filling out a form and running off. I've won an expensive Miele vacuum cleaner and an iPad at shows – for the iPad there were only five names in the draw.

Tips

- Always take a pen with you – don't waste time waiting for the person in front of you to finish writing.

- Take a smartphone with a QR reader – for some draws you have to scan codes.

- Flick through the brochure/guide as soon as you arrive – some stands will advertise their comps in the brochure – circle their stands on your floor plan and be sure to visit them.

- Check Twitter for the show hashtag – look for companies who are tweeting comps. At one show I attended, the company tweeted they were offering a prize for *"the first person to come to our stand and say 'chicken lips'!"*

- Do your research – check the Facebook page and Twitter feed of the show organisers to see what promotions are going on.

- For trade shows, take plenty of business cards – if you don't have a job you could get some printed cheaply with a job title like 'Social Media Manager' (well, you do manage your own Facebook account, right?). If your partner has business cards, drop those in the boxes too. You'll still see a lot of 'fish bowl' prize draws in hotels and restaurants too, so it's always worth having a few cards in your bag.

- Smile and be friendly – one man I spoke to said they always pick the most unusual business card as the winner. Show the reps your business card or your name badge, they might well remember you and decide they want you to win… naughty, but true.

- After the show, keep your brochures and check the listed exhibitors' Facebook and Twitter pages for comps – these will probably be brands that compers don't know about, so you might find some low entry promotions that way.

29. Look for experiential events

Experiential marketing is where a brand creates an 'experience' for the consumer – it might be a pop-up café or a huge installation in a shopping centre. You might see these events advertised on social media or in local papers – or you could stumble across an event whilst shopping. In the UK, **www.promomarketing.info** is good for a heads-up on future promotional activity.

Some of the teams who work at events like this are actually pretty poor at approaching consumers – so it pays for you to be confident and ask about prizes. If you see the latest car model in a shopping centre, smile and ask nicely if there's a competition involved. These days it's less likely to be an entry form and more likely to be a social media share in the form of a tweet or photo. They might want you to film a fun video, take a selfie with the car or tweet a hashtag to take part. I spotted a Smart Car demo in my local shopping centre, tweeted a selfie and within an hour I got a Twitter Direct Message saying I'd won a £10 voucher – fast work!

49

Busy city train stations often have experiential campaigns set up. British Airways have hosted two generous promotions at London stations where they gave away a pair of worldwide flights every hour. To win, you had to get the hour's best score by landing the plane using a flight simulator. As you can imagine, the odds of winning were fantastic and several SuperLucky readers won flights to the Caribbean.

I read online about a Zanussi promotion where they were touring their new range at various electrical stores in the UK – there was an appliance to be won at every venue, and entry forms had to be completed and handed in on the day. I arrived in the late afternoon and the lady told me she had less than five entries. I won a washing machine, of course!

You might wonder if it's worth your while going out of the way to attend an event, but from experience it's *always* a fun thing to do, even if you lose – I've had some hilarious moments snatching golden tickets from the air in shopping centres.

Treasure hunts where clues are revealed on a website, Facebook, Twitter or the radio are a fun way to win prizes if you're flexible with time and have access to transport. I won an expensive Alexander McQueen scarf by being the first person to arrive at Nottingham's Old Market Square and utter the magic phrase "Muller Light" – and there was even a treasure hunt on Twitter where a lucky guy won a prize car after tracking it down to Clacton seafront.

30. Subscribe to a listings magazine

Once you've decided comping is the hobby for you, you might be prepared to invest a little money into it. In the UK there are two dedicated magazines for competition listings, *Simply Prizes* and *Compers News*, both available only by subscription. The prices vary, with occasional special offers, but you're currently looking at a cost of around £60 by annual direct debit.

So what can you expect from a magazine? Hundreds of competitions, ranging from postal entry to purchase necessary, text comps and creative comps. In addition, there are plenty of reader-only prize draws and competitions. As well as getting a printed copy in the post, you'll be able to access an online digital edition (with clickable links) about a week before you receive the magazine.

Critics of competition listings magazine are usually those who have never read them. If you don't mind paying to enter the odd competition – and by this I mean sending a standard rate text or buying a can of pop – then you'll find a magazine like *Compers News* brilliant. If you're more of a money-saving comper, then a magazine probably won't be your thing. If you're not sure, you could always ask for a subscription for your birthday and give it a try!

Compers News

When I first started coming regularly back in the 1990s, Compers News Chatterbox was the first coming forum I found online. I subscribed to the monthly newsletter and was hooked! Back then it was a simple text only newsletter, featuring the occasional reader's letter. In the years since, it's merged with several other competition magazines including Competitor's Companion, Prize Draw Winner and Competition Grapevine, and is now a full colour magazine. As well as the *Listings File*, featuring hundreds of competitions, there are reader stories, news, advice, exclusive puzzles and much more – I even have my own monthly column sharing tips on coming online.

In my opinion, the best benefit of a Compers News subscription is immediate access to the online Chatterbox forum. As you can imagine, some comps have a very short life and with the time it takes to print a magazine, they can't be included – the Chatterbox forum is a great resource for these short-lived low entry comps. The editor, Steve Middleton, has been comping enthusiastically since the 1970s and works tirelessly to find prize promotions with low entry numbers – his expertise is in tracking down purchase-necessary and instant win promotions as soon as they hit the shelves, and sharing the details with Chatterbox members.

Six month subscriptions to Compers News start from £29.70 using my affiliate link at **www.superlucky.me/SubscribeCN**.

Simply Prizes

Although Simply Prizes magazine doesn't have a chat forum, it does give members access to extra competitions via the website at **www.simplyprizes.com**.

If you do decide to subscribe to a magazine, make sure you enter the reader-only competitions and email in your winning stories and photos, no matter how trivial they might seem! You'll have a good chance of winning a voucher, cash or stamps with your contribution, and with a few wins each year, could even cover the cost of your subscription.

31. Join a local comp club

Comp clubs and get-togethers are an excellent way of finding out about new promotions – you'll leave the meetings motivated and inspired, usually with a bulging bag of magazines and entry forms.

I'll never forget my first experience of a compers' meeting – it was in the early 2000s at a fabulous event known as *Big Brum*, organised by Birmingham comp club, Kompers Korner. Over a hundred compers gathered annually to exchange entry forms, chat and enter fun competitions, with a massive charity raffle to end the day. I went alone to the first Big Brum and chatted to several other compers – we had a great time, and it was a relief for me to find people who finally understood the strange hobby I'd taken up!

Not long afterwards I joined the Compers News chat forum and went to a members' meeting near my house in Nottingham – there were about 20 of us there, including comping legend Brita Bevis. I met a group of ladies that day who remain some of my closest friends. Meeting compers in real life is inspiring and fun, and it certainly helps you to win prizes when you work as a team! Soon I was invited to join the Toton comp club (with Compers News columnist Pam Crampton), started a comp club in North Notts (with Compers News editor Steve), and joined the *Notts about Comping* group. Now I'm a member of *Brighton Breezy* down on the South Coast, meeting with like-minded wine-loving compers every three weeks.

I'm also a member of the *London Competitor's Club* (LCC) – anyone is welcome to join the club without having to attend the London meetings, and will receive a quarterly newsletter and access to the email group. It's currently £17.50 for a year and you can find out more about joining at **www.compelation.co.uk**.

These days the bigger comping days are few and far between – the LCC has quarterly meetings for members and guests, and you can still find events occasionally in Manchester, Yorkshire and the South-West. If you're interested in American conventions you can check *Contest Queen* Carolyn Wilman's list at **www.superlucky. me/SweepsConventions**.

Local comp clubs are still popular, but it can be difficult to find information on venues and times – see **www.superlucky.me/ CompClubs** for my up-to-date list of UK clubs. If there's not one near you, check the comments to see if you can find any local friends who might want to start one up.

Meeting formats

All comp clubs work differently. A few smaller clubs hold meetings in members' houses on rotation, but most will be in a pub or café. They can be as often as fortnightly, or organised on a whim every six months! It's rare for members to make it to every meeting, and new members or guests are usually welcome. Comp club meetings are relaxed and informal, but there may be rotas set at the beginning of the year to decide who's responsible for bringing raffle prizes. Here's what generally happens:

- **Wins** – members take turns to say what they've won since the last meeting.

- **Prize draws** – members may bring magazines (with entry forms in), *quallies* (promotional products where a receipt is required for entry) or stamped postcards to be given away in prize draws.

- **Entry forms** – members bring along any entry forms, free magazines and newspapers, or photocopies of current competitions, usually bundled into sets ready to be distributed between club members.

- **Quizzes** – members might take turns in setting a quiz.

- **Comping chat** – members sometimes need advice on Facebook, Twitter or a certain competition – or simply need a bit of motivation to get going after a comping break!

"I love my comp club meetings because it gives me inspiration to hear what my friends have won that month – there's always a big win (or two or three!). We share news of the latest comps, and will go the extra mile to get a competition qualifier for the members if they're not near a shop. We've made really good friends and it's lovely to catch up with their lives and families too!" –
Laura Farnworth

---

32. Look out for litter

There are often prize promotions on chocolate wrappers, crisp packets and drinks bottles – and if, like me, you live near a secondary school, you're likely to find promotional ones discarded all over the local park by littering teenagers. I simply can't walk past a piece of litter if the word 'Win' is grinning back at me – my hairdresser always laughs about the first time I visited the salon and immediately retrieved a promotional Kettle Chips packet from her bin!

'Wombling' for codes is great because you're helping to rid your neighbourhood of litter *and* getting a chance to win a prize. If you have a baby or toddler, it's easy to tuck discarded promotional bottles and wrappers discreetly into the bottom of your pushchair without looking too much like a mad woman. Don't take it too far though; think twice about taking things out of bins and consider the health and safety aspect.

Make sure you know the details of current *purchase necessary* promotions (a magazine like Compers News is great for this) and keep an eye out for litter when you're out and about. For some promotions (check first!), you don't need to keep hold of the promotional packaging, so you can take a photo of the code on your phone, then bin or recycle the wrapper or bottle.

In the UK, Lucozade have an ongoing promotion called the YES project. Each promotional bottle has a unique code printed under the wrapper with a chance to win hourly prizes when you input the code at **www.lucozadeenergy.com**. In addition, Cadbury, Walkers, Coke, KitKat and Kinder Bueno often feature codes on the packaging.

You can womble for receipts as well as packaging – if you use apps like *Shopitize* or *CheckoutSmart*, you'll earn cashback and prize draw entries for uploading supermarket receipts. It's not just small prizes that you can win with a bit of wombling. Back in the 2000s, you had to spend £10 at a Spar in order to enter a tiebreaker competition to win a car. My friend collected discarded receipts from trolleys at her local Spar and shared them with our comping group – we were delighted when our member Julie won the car!

"It was 'wombling' that introduced me to comping in 1970. I was a student and on my way home one very rainy afternoon my eye was caught by an empty box of Macleans toothpaste with the word WIN on the side. Despite being very wet and soggy in the gutter I picked it up, had a go at the slogan and sent it in. Amazingly I won a holiday to the Algarve – my first ever trip by plane. I screamed so loudly when I opened the LWE that all my housemates thought something awful had happened!" – Janet Leng

---

33. Search for contestant calls

Quiz shows and game shows give away massive amounts of prize money – in the UK the winnings are tax free but in the US you will have to pay tax on the prizes. If you're confident under pressure, flexible with recording dates, and have a lively personality, you could be a great candidate for a TV game show or quiz.

Despite what you might think, it's not that difficult to get on a show – especially a brand new one. I recorded a new show *Ejector Seat* in 2014. They interviewed 3,000 applicants nationwide and needed 300 for the show – an impressive 1-in-10 chance of getting on. Also, there's no need to panic – it really isn't as scary as it looks. I used to be terrified of doing anything in public – it was when I got into comping I realised there were prizes out there that could only be won if you were brave enough to call up a radio station or appear on TV.

To get on a show you need to respond to *contestant calls*, which you can find on **www.beonscreen.com**, **www.bbc.co.uk**, **www.itv.com/**

beontv, www.starnow.co.uk and **ukgameshows.com**. If you're on Twitter, follow **@officialcastme, @starnow** or **@tvcastingplus** who all tweet requests. If you spot a good show advertised, send an email (you usually get an immediate automated response with an attached entry form) or complete an online application form. Sometimes you'll be able to record a video application using your webcam or phone.

New shows will get less applications than long-running, famous shows like *Deal or No Deal* as people aren't actively looking to apply. You'll also see requests for people to film a one-off pilot show – this may or may not involve a cash prize, but is worth applying for as it's good practice and participants are often invited back to record the real thing if it gets commissioned.

Once you've found a show worth applying for, read my advice on how to handle the auditions and filming in **Get on a game show** (tip 69).

Tips for entering competitions

You should now have plenty of ideas for *finding* competitions, but next you need to *enter* them efficiently and correctly. In this section you'll find practical guidance on organising your comping routine, plus the best ways to enter different types of prize promotion.

34. Make time for comping

One of the main reasons people don't try comping is because they think it's so time-consuming, but it doesn't have to be. Anyone, no matter how busy, can incorporate a little comping into their life – you just need to be organised enough to fit it in around everything else, and take advantage of every spare moment.

If you walk the kids to school, check your phone for Twitter comps on the way back. If you drive to school or work, listen to the radio – there are always comps on the breakfast and drivetime shows worth pulling over for. Your lunch break at the office can be a great time to jump onto Twitter or Facebook and do a few quick comps. If you're early for a meeting, why not pop into the newsagent and check the local paper for comps?

Some people prefer to get up early in the morning to enter their comps – that's a great time to be doing instant wins. Other compers enjoy burning the midnght oil – that's a good time to do the Facebook likes, shares and comments as you won't be invading your friends' news feed with your comps. Got a new baby? Your iPhone should be your best friend during those night feeds!

"I have a five-month-old daughter, and have had a successful year from comping in the night whilst feeding – a great way to stop myself falling asleep. Win win!" –
Alex T

58

You should be thinking about comping *every time* you walk into the supermarket too – don't just pick up the items on your shopping list, try to pop down every aisle and check for on-pack promotions. Teach the kids to spot the magic word *'Win'*!

If you're struggling to find time for comps, your first step should be to organise your home and family life – meal planning, de-cluttering and organising family zones can reduce the amount of time you have to spend cleaning, tidying and cooking – and free up valuable comping time. My good friend Jo has a wonderful membership site, *The Inspired Mama Revolution,* which can help you organise your life and make time for the fun stuff – check it out at **www.my-organized-chaos.com**.

Comping is the perfect hobby to do in front of the TV in the evenings too – luckily Rob is a Twitter addict, so he can't really complain when I sit there tapping away on my laptop!

35. Autofill entry forms

We all lead busy lives, and who wants to waste time manually typing information into online forms, or typing in usernames and passwords every day for the same websites? Luckily, most browsers now offer to automatically complete your details in online forms – type the first few letters and your browser will complete the rest. You can also choose to save login and password details for websites.

If you use Chrome, it automatically saves the information that you enter into a form (name, address, phone number, email address, etc.). Add or edit your details by going to the Chrome menu (three lines at the top right of the browser window), then *Settings*, scrolling down to *Show Advanced Settings*, then *Manage Autofill Settings* or *Manage Passwords*.

When you start filling out a form, the Autofill entries that match what you're typing appear in a menu, and you select an entry to complete the form. Chrome also saves the text you've typed in specific fields on a form – for example the answer to a question or a barcode number on a daily entry prize draw. The next time you fill out that field, text that you've typed in the past appears – select the text you want from the menu.

In Internet Explorer, the function is called *AutoComplete* – click the *Tools* button, then *Internet options* – on the *Content* tab, under AutoComplete, tap or click *Settings* and select the option to complete forms.

If you fill out a lot of entry forms – particularly lengthy ones with unusual questions or fields – consider downloading the brilliant **RoboForm** (tip 71) for its custom fields.

36. Set up keyboard shortcuts

Keyboard shortcuts for text are fantastic timesavers, yet most people don't know they exist. You can create and customise any shortcut you like, and it's perfect for your name, address, phone number, email and other details you're constantly typing. For Mac users, iCloud will synchonise any shortcut you create to all your devices.

Here's how to set up Keyboard Shortcuts on an iPhone:

- Tap *Settings > General > Keyboard.*

- Scroll down to *Shortcuts.*

- Tap *Add New Shortcut...*

- In the Phrase field, type in the entire phrase you'd like to create a shortcut for, eg. *12 Stanley Road, London SW5 3RT* or *jo.smith798@gmail.com* – or even *'Liked and shared'!*

- In the *Shortcut* field, type in the snippet you want to be replaced by the phrase, *eg. 12s* or *jo.*

- Tap *Save.*

To use a shortcut just type your short phrase, and tap the space bar. Your long phrase will appear! Set a shortcut for text competitions that require your name, house number, postcode and email address – it's a great timesaver.

On an Android phone, go to *Settings > Language & Input > Personal dictionary* to set your shortcuts. For PC users, **AutoHotKey** is a great bit of free software to use to write 'scripts' for your shortcuts.

My shortcuts

- **di.** – when I type this, my email address appears

- **07** – when I type this, my phone number appears

- **40i** – when I type this, my entire address and postcode appears

- **sl** – when I type this, the web address http://superlucky.me appears

Other tips

- Does your local radio station always ask for the same format when you text in – perhaps a keyword and your name? Set up a shortcut for that and yours will always be the first text message to arrive.

- I find myself tweeting promoters with *'Where are the T&Cs and closing date please?'* so often, I made that into a shortcut too!

- If you regularly comment on Facebook comps, or reply to RT comps, set up a few standard phrases you can use, eg. a shortcut of *lp* could type *'Lovely prize – thanks for the giveaway!'* which would save you lots of time.

37. Enter lots of times

Whether it's tweeting daily for a Gleam giveaway, entering an hourly instant win or sending a weekly text message – getting more than one entry in the draw gives you the best possible chance of a win, and it's worth doing if it's a prize you really want.

You will usually find one of these statements in the promotion terms and conditions, sometimes followed by *'per day'*:

- **One entry per household** – one person at your address can enter once.

- **One entry per person** – every person in your household/family can enter once.

- **One entry per email address** – if you have multiple email addresses, you can enter with all of them.

- **One entry per mobile phone number** – if you have multiple phone numbers, you can enter with all of them.

If you're entering a *'one entry per household'* draw online, your IP address (the location of your computer) will usually be recorded, and any further entries from that IP address will be disqualified.

In the case of *'one entry per phone number'* or *'one entry per email address'* promotions, gain an advantage by using multiple SIM cards in phone handsets, and setting up a number of email addresses.

Some purchase necessary promotions specify you can enter once per day, but you don't *always* need to make a separate purchase for each day. Check the rules carefully to see what has to be provided if you win – if you have to input a barcode or batch code from the packaging, you may be able to enter the same code every day. It's rare that a promoter actually asks for a receipt corresponding to each of your daily entries, so you may be prepared to risk it.

On the other hand, if the product has a unique code and you need a different code for every entry then you should consider buying in bulk – a good idea if it's a product with a long shelf life or that can be distributed amongst family and friends. Buy as much as you can without feeling guilty: £50 spent on M&Ms might seem crazy but if you win a holiday then it's worth it – and don't forget, you have the chocolate too! Check at **www.mysupermarket.co.uk** to see where the promotional products are cheapest – or find a friend with a Cash & Carry card. Promo packs don't always stay on the shelves for the entire duration of a promotion, so stock up early and save your codes to enter at the end of the promotion.

If you really want to win a certain prize (tickets for example) you could ask your closest comping friends to enter on your behalf – this is a great tactic if it's something they have no interest in. Check the T&Cs though – if the prize is not transferable, don't do it.

If it's a text competition that allows one entry per mobile number – and even better, one entry per day per mobile number – charge up any old handsets you have and pop a free Pay-As-You-Go (PAYG) SIM card into them.

If you're entering social media comps multiple times, your actions might be seen as spamming, so be careful. Multiple retweets, Facebook shares or use of the same hashtag repeatedly can result in you getting filtered out of Twitter searches, or even a Facebook commenting ban. On the other hand, if rules state you can enter a photo competition unlimited times – go for it! Most people will only enter once, and you'll stand out as being super keen.

For Gleam and Rafflecopter giveaways, entrants are usually rewarded with bonus draw entries for a daily tweet, so make the most of it.

Some years back, when postcard comps were more common, I won a week's holiday to Japan with *Now* magazine by posting off a carefully handmade Japanese themed postcard every day until the closing date. My dedication resulted in a £10,000 holiday to Tokyo – it was well worth the cost of sending 10 postcards.

38. Enter postal competitions

Postcard competitions are rare these days, but you can still find them listed in Compers News magazine, and a few on special boards within the Loquax and Money Saving Expert forums. There are postal entry routes for comps in magazines and newspapers, and kids' comics and magazines are a good source.

If a prize draw or competition has multiple prizes, the promoter will usually split those between entry routes. The most popular entry route will be the free one – for example, email or via a website. There will be fewer entries via text or post, giving you a better chance of a win if you've sent a postcard.

An error in a magazine competition can work in your favour if you're entering by post. Even if the mistake means your entry is incomplete (eg. Only circling 5 'spot the differences' when there should be 6) it's still worth a stamp as a large majority of people won't bother sending their forms off at all. I spotted a mistake in the Q magazine crossword, and scribbled a cheeky comment along with the correct answer on my entry form. I won £1,000 of shopping vouchers.

Postcards

If a competition requires entry on a postcard, send your details on a plain postcard (promotion address on the front, your details on the back), a picture postcard (promotion address on the right, yours on the left), or a homemade postcard. If you write both addresses on one side of the card, write your own address at a 90 degree angle, and run the postcode on from your city name. This will reduce the risk of your entry being returned to you because the machine has scanned the wrong postcode – see an example at **www.superlucky. me/PostcardDraws**.

You can find free picture postcards at bars and restaurants, and I've found some quirky blank vintage postcards at car boot sales and on eBay. Most of the postcards I send are the front of old greetings cards, or homemade from brightly coloured card. I used to send giant homemade funny shaped postcards covered in sticky foam, googly eyes and all sorts of tat, but these days I imagine they would cost a fortune to send, and cause mayhem if they got stuck in Royal Mail's machines!

Some compers swear by using small address stickers on their postcards. Handling houses (big companies that handle the responses to promotions, usually via a PO Box address) probably approve, as it means less chance of errors, but I tend to think smaller companies would be put off by such comping professionalism.

If there are a number of postcard entry draws in the same publication, sometimes you can send your postcards AIOE (all in one envelope) and just pay postage once for the envelope. It's best to contact the magazine before you post your entries, to find out if this is acceptable – your envelope may move into the more expensive *large letter* zone if it's 5mm thick, so do check.

Big national publications like the Daily Express offer a choice of expensive text entry or cheaper postal entry for some prize draws – people tend to presume the telephone entrants have a better chance of winning, but I've heard of holiday and car winners entering via the postal route, so it's worth doing.

Entry forms

Entry form competitions are rare, but offer a great chance of a prize. Pop the form into a plain envelope and send off, or do as I do and stick it onto a postcard to make your entry stand out. Look out for entry forms in women's weeklies and kids' magazines.

Stamps and envelopes

Buy envelopes in bulk – C6 size is the most practical. Coloured envelopes and stickers can be a winner, especially for local prize draws – many of my comping friends have had success with a gold envelope! Another tip is to use pretty stamps – the Royal Mail prints sheets of themed stamps, and occasionally you can pick up second class ones. They really make envelopes and postcards stand out. If there's a price rise imminent, stock up on your stamps as soon as you can – and watch out for Superdrug discounts in the UK, they sometimes give you 5% off stamp books.

39. Text to win

There are plenty of text/SMS promotions around, many of them offering huge life-changing prizes. You'll find them advertised in magazines and newspapers, on radio, TV or on products. Occasionally you might spot one advertised at the *point of sale* – a stand, poster or shelf label in your local supermarket or convenience store. Sometimes these in-store text promotions aren't publicised widely at all and can be surprisingly low entry – the posters might only appear a few days before the closing date.

Check the small print to see the cost of sending the text – in some cases it can be as high as £2. Consider whether you really want to spend that much on a prize draw! For the pricey text promotions, you may get a message back tempting you into sending another entry to get a third free – but don't get carried away. Text comps aren't *always* expensive though – in many cases the message will be SR (standard rate) or even free on your phone tariff.

For text comps, you rarely need to send much more than a keyword or name – so you could put a new Pay-As-You-Go SIM card into a few old phone handsets, and enter multiple times. Use as many phones as you can handle – some compers will assign one phone to each of their family members, while others actually use more than ten to maximise their chances.

Personally, I find text competitions incredibly boring. I send off the odd entry, but I just can't get into the habit of making daily entries, or keeping a variety of handsets fully charged up, yet this commitment will give you the best chance of picking up prizes. Having said that, I did win a £1,000 Eurocamp holiday in a text comp. This was a generous prize draw advertised on a Nestlé cereals packet, and each month for three months they gave away 75 holidays. These are the type of comps it's worth paying the cost of a phone call or text message to enter as there are so many prizes! Keep in mind that most people will pour the cereal out, glance at the competition but not do anything about it as they're eating and nowhere near a phone – but there's nothing I like more at breakfast time than studying T&Cs on a yogurt pot or cereal box!

Around ten years ago I read on the Compers News chat forum that Nutrigrain bars had launched a text-to-win promotion to win £500 every hour, and each wrapper was printed with a unique code. There was a real buzz about it amongst compers, so I thought I'd give it a go. I bought about ten boxes of bars and set my alarm for 3am in the hope that nobody else would be daft enough to text their codes at that time – and hit gold. Rob and I won six £500 cash prizes in total over two weeks – I'd spent over £100 on chewy bars and barely slept, but it was worth it to get the cash I needed for our new kitchen!

"Way back in the day Di told me about a competition where you had to buy the product and text the code. I was setting my alarm hourly in the middle of the night. It was hilarious and tiring but worth it when I won the cash!" – Lisa Barr

40. Have fun with Facebook

Facebook is an amazing source of competitions, and if you really want to make a go of your hobby, you should dive in headfirst. Lots of compers don't like Facebook or Twitter at all, meaning that comps on these social networks get fewer entries than web prize draws. When it comes to Facebook promotions, you can either find them on an *app* or a *timeline*.

Facebook apps

Facebook apps range from simple entry forms and instant win games, to photo galleries and leaderboard challenges. To enter most of them you'll either need to give the app permission to access your email address (and possibly other information from your public Facebook profile), or simply complete your name and email in an entry form. In either of these situations, you can be assured the promoter has access to your email address and *hopefully* will contact you via email if you win.

Timeline promotions

Every Facebook page and user has their own *timeline* of events, presented in reverse chronological order. Brand pages like to host competitions and prize draws on their timeline to encourage interaction with their fans. There are a few ways to enter a timeline promotion on Facebook:

- **Like the competition post** – simply click the thumbs up button.

- **Comment on the competition post** – type your comment in the empty box underneath the photo or post. The promoter may ask a question or specify what you should comment, or you may be free to post what you like.

- **Comment on the competition post with a link or photo** – Click the camera icon to upload a photo to your comment (this function isn't activated on some brand pages). If you add a web link, your comment will include a preview of that website.

- **Share a post or photo to the timeline** – this is where, rather than commenting on an existing post, you create your own post or share a photo on the brand page – usually with a competition hashtag.

- **Email entry** – some promotions are advertised in a Facebook post, but to enter you have to send an email.

- **Like the page** – Facebook terms of use don't allow incentivised page likes, but promoters tend to ignore that and still ask entrants to Like their pages in order to enter.

- **Share** – Asking entrants to share as a condition of entry is a breach of Facebook terms of use. If you do enter share comps, you should always share on the *Public* setting. Shares to *Friends*, *Only Me* or restricted lists – or shares to closed

68

or private groups – will *not* be seen by the promoter. Having said that, most compers believe that the promoters don't even look at the shares list, and will choose from Likes/Comments instead. See the **Learn to keep a secret** section (tip 58) for more on sharing settings.

If you're entering Facebook like or comment comps, check that you're actually commenting on the original post – not on your friend's share of the post. From a news feed or timeline, click the photo to open up the original post.

"I recently won a Go Pro on Facebook – you had to describe your dad in three words. I added a rather funny photo of him – some promoters seem to like an image being added even if they only ask you to answer with a comment!" – Christina Curtis

---

41. Write slogans and rhymes

It's not a crime to rhyme! Rhyming couplets are what most older compers still associate with our hobby – from the 1950s to the early 2000s, tiebreaker or slogan competitions were ever so popular. Indeed, in 2000 there was a point where a trip to Sainsbury's resulted in eight or more different orange entry forms where a purchase and a tiebreaker was required. Those were the days! Now though, it's rare to find a slogan competition – and even if you do find one, the winners may be chosen at random rather than by a panel of judges discussing the most 'apt and original' answer. The method of concocting fun rhymes can still be applied to today's prize draws and competitions – you can incorporate slogans into a tweet or Facebook comment. A promoter looking through a long list of similar, dull responses might well smile if they see a fun rhyme in the midst of it all! They also work brilliantly for occasions such as Valentine's Day (adding a funny twist to 'Roses are red, violets are blue' for example), Mother's Day and Father's Day.

I've had plenty of success with slogans myself – one of my favourites was *'Feeling jolly, filled my trolley, Deck the halls with sprouts and cauli!'*, which won me £500 of Morrisons vouchers. My prize VW Beetle was won with *'From winter woollies to skimpy underwear, Zanussi technology is programmed to care!'*, and *'For central heating in tip-top condition, Fernox is always in Pole Position!'* won me a trip to the Brazilian Grand Prix. My tiebreaker technique is rather rusty now, but I do love the chance to do a bit of rhyming once in a while.

Tiebreaker tips

- **Brainstorm.** Jot down – either on paper or electronically – all the ideas, words and phrases that come to mind when you think of the promoter, product and prize. Choose key words and work them into your slogan or poem.

- **Be positive and upbeat.** In most cases, sob stories will get you nowhere in a judged competition. Being funny isn't always appropriate for a tiebreaker, but in most cases if your wordplay and puns make the judges chuckle you're in with a good chance of winning.

- **Read the rules.** It might seem obvious, but have a really good read of the terms and conditions – if there are any. Make sure you don't go over the maximum word limit – because if you do, and you go on to win, you can guarantee an eagle-eyed comper will point it out to the promoter and your prize may be withdrawn. If a competition has detailed T&Cs, chances are that they've included some form of criteria which the tiebreaker entries will be judged on – check this against the main website or Facebook information. On Facebook there might be a landing page for an app that says 'the funniest entry will win', but T&Cs state the 'most creative and original' entry will win. If that's the case, you should make sure that yours is creative, original AND funny!

- **Keep it short and snappy.** Just because you can write up to 150 words, doesn't mean you should. A shorter entry may work to your advantage amongst all the rambling prose. To check your word count, copy and paste your entry in at **www. wordcounter.net** – or if you're tweeting, type it into the tweet box to check how many characters you have to play with. If you use Microsoft Word, you can use Word Count from the drop down menu in Review.

- **Find rhyming words.** Use a rhyming dictionary, or **www. rhymezone.com**, which also has a synonym option if you can't quite find the right word. You can download the Rhymezone mobile app, but it will cost you £2.29.

- **Use the Windex.** If you're a Compers News subscriber you can access an excellent resource called the Windex at **www.compersnews.com**, and search over 60,000 winning competition slogans for inspiration. It's excellent at brainstorming stage, but don't copy existing slogans – if someone spots it, you'll be left red-faced!

- **Read it out loud.** If you've written a rhyme, check the scansion (rhythm) by reading it out loud – it should have the same number of syllables in each line. You may need to change or remove a word to make it sound better.

- **Be topical.** Promoters like to see something original, and if your entry is topical and references current sporting events, celebrities or news it proves you haven't just copied something from Google.

- **Enter caption competitions.** I've never been much good at writing captions, but if you're quick-thinking and good with jokes and puns, go for it!

Lots of tiebreaker and caption competitions are quick ones hosted on Facebook or Twitter, so unfortunately it's not possible to spend ages perfecting a clever answer – just ensure you make a good first impression, as the judge might not spend much time choosing the winner. A lot of competitions state that winners will be chosen at random, while the quality of the winning entries suggests they were judged. Put as much time into writing your entry as you can spare – just in case.

42. Call up the radio

I started freelancing from home ten years ago, and it wasn't long after that I discovered the delights of radio competitions. Back then cash prizes were common on my local stations, and they regularly gave away fantastic holidays. These days the sponsors aren't quite as generous, but it's still an enjoyable way to win prizes – and a quick way to get your competition fix.

I remember driving home listening to Trent FM a few years ago when they asked for callers to identify a song in a second to win £1,000. I pulled into a layby, got through straight away on my mobile, and recognised the first three notes of a Jamelia song. It was the fastest and easiest £1,000 I ever earnt! I won another £1,000 a few weeks later for solving the Nottingham Tram Treasure Trail (which involved me inspecting trees in a local park), and have won three holidays, a Smeg fridge and over £5,000 in cash from other stations including Gold, TalkSport, Absolute, Kerrang!, Heart, Magic and Smooth.

Before the promotion is on-air, find out the studio number, programme it into your phone memory and prepare your phone, so that you only need to press one button to dial. If you have a spare handset (compers often have many of these with 'Pay-as-you-go' SIMs) then use two phones to call. If possible, listen to the station on a proper old-fashioned radio (or car radio), not the internet or digital TV because of the delay. When you hear the promoter begin to introduce the competition, start calling straight away. The phone will hopefully ring, but if it's engaged then keep redialling for a few minutes. Often they need a couple of callers and may put you on hold just in case the first caller messes up. If the phone does ring and isn't answered, don't hang up until you hear them talking again on the radio.

If the phone is answered, sound excited, enthusiastic and friendly – and it's difficult, but try not to sound too nervous.

If it's an on-air quiz, you can gain an advantage if you have someone at home to help you out (most stations don't mind this as long as you admit it if asked!). I make sure I'm sitting with my MacBook so if I'm stuck I can quickly Google for the answers. If your friends are also tuning in, work as a team in a Facebook chat or group – you can help each other with answers. If it's a head to head you could also strike a deal with a friend: some stations do a daily quiz where the winner stays on. Get your friend to phone up and lose and that will buy you another day. This works better with local stations as so few people call up!

Even if you're not sure what the answer is, it's worth calling in to the studio. One competition I vividly recall entering was a national radio promotion. The station had a set of 100 music questions and each hour a caller was brought on air and randomly given three of them. I got through several times and kept getting two out of three. Eventually the DJ told me off-air they *had* to give the prize away, informing me the answer I needed was *Fall Out Boy*. We went on to re-record my call as if I'd given the right answer first time! Rather naughty, but as I was £1,000 richer I wasn't complaining. If you do get on air and don't win, then don't despair – you've been brave enough to try and the next time you won't feel as nervous. I'll never forget the time I lost out on a £10,000 kitchen because I didn't guess that George Clooney was the mystery celebrity – I can laugh about it now but at the time I was devastated!

Preparation is key with radio comps. Tune in on Monday to see how the competition works and what time the phone lines are opened. Do your research on the film, holiday destination or event – you'll find lots of statistics on Wikipedia. When Rob's football team (Arsenal) and mine (Birmingham City) met in the League Cup I knew we'd win tickets. TalkSport were giving away a pair daily in a head-to-head on air quiz. The first day they asked lots of hard questions about the teams, scores and matches played in the run up to the final. I registered Rob and myself online, printed off a list of statistics and crossed my fingers. Next day, Rob got the call to go on air, swotted up and got all his answers right. We won the tickets – and, against all odds, Birmingham won the match!

"I often listen out for radio competitions – I prefer ones that you can call in on rather than text as I feel your chances of getting picked are quite slim. My recent win for a weekend away in London through Magic FM was something I was determined to get through on, and I got through on the last day of the week – I was very happy!"- Vanessa Alvis

---

43. Enter purchase-necessary promotions

Many compers choose to keep their hobby 'free', only entering online competitions and draws – and that's fine because there are *thousands* of free prize draws and competitions online. But venture into text, phone, postal and proof of purchase (POP) required promotions and you'll find they can be very rewarding. I've won holidays, cash and voucher prizes in *purchase-necessary* comps – in fact I'd rather spend £2 on a stamp, a phone call, a promotional KitKat and a newspaper than a Lottery ticket, because the chance of winning a prize is so much better. The more expensive the qualifying purchase, the fewer people will enter and the better your chance of winning. My most expensive qualifier was a washing machine – but it ended up winning me a VW Beetle, so it was money well spent!

On-pack promotions

Most on-pack promotions include a unique code (or PIN) printed somewhere on the packaging. It may be visible on a neck collar, or printed onto a bottle (eg. Lucozade Yes Project), under a label or on a sticker. The codes are entered online – or sometimes via text. Hidden codes offer the best chance of winning – when codes are freely available on neck collars or stickers, cheeky compers can easily swipe extra ones in the supermarket, or even write down the codes to use.

If you put your promotional packs away in the cupboard, you risk a family member using them and throwing the packaging away before you've entered the comp. I always note down unique codes immediately and carefully using Evernote on my iPhone, along with the web address or text entry details and the final closing date of the promotion. If I wake up early, I enter a handful of instant win comps by simply copying and pasting the codes from my list. If your codes include unrecognisable digits, snap a photo on your phone (this can be filed in Evernote, Drive or Dropbox) and read the code from this photo when you need it, trying different combinations until you get it right!

There are several types of on-pack code promotions, the most common are:

Winning moment (instant win)

For the first type of 'winning moment', the first entry received after the randomly generated 'winning moment' will bag the prize – it could be seconds afterwards, or hours afterwards. There could be one winning moment in a week, or a hundred a day! If there is no entry between one winning moment and the next, two prizes will usually be awarded after the next winning moment instead, so all prizes are awarded. Sometimes, if a prize isn't won it will be offered in a prize draw for all losing entries at the end of the promotion.

For the second type, you actually need to enter *during* the winning moment rather than afterwards – it could be a moment that's just one second long! For these, only a small percentage of the prizes will be given away. An example is the recent McDonald's Monopoly promotion, where there was a winning moment every minute – you had to enter during that exact moment to win a prize. Winning moment comps usually require a code from a promotional pack, but not always. If you win, you'll get the winning notification immediately, either online, by email or by text.

Winning code (instant win)

For the first type of winning code, all winning codes are pre-assigned and printed onto packs. Usually, unless the winning code is entered into the competition, the prize will not be won – although occasionally some nice promoters might offer the unclaimed prizes in a prize draw after the competition ends. These promotions will always seem very generous – eg. a recent Rachel's Organic promotion had 10,000 Royal Doulton prizes to win, although only a handful were actually claimed. Compers often call this an *instant lose* promotion, and there was much controversy when the New Covent Garden Soup Company didn't give away the £500,000 farm they promoted widely on their boxes – because the winning code was never entered on the website.

For the second type, each code on packaging has an equal chance of being a winner. Odds will be decided in advance – eg. 10,000,000 crisp packets are printed with the promotional codes on and there are 1,000 prizes. In this example, when you input your code, a computer program will assign your entry a unique number which would have a 1-in-10,000 chance of winning. In this case, the codes on packaging may not be unique – you could be required to input the batch and time code from your pack. Again – if your code is a winner, you'll get the winning notification immediately, either online, by email or by text.

Prize draw

For some promotions, you enter your unique code via text or online for a prize draw rather than an instant win. There may be hourly or daily prizes, or perhaps just one draw for a big holiday prize. For some promotions, as well as having a chance at an instant win prize you're also entered into a draw for a grand prize – eg. Yeo Valley recently ran an instant win promotion for a camper van, but all losing entries went into a draw for a second camper van. For 'Rewards Club' promotions, codes from packs are required and can be exchanged for prize draw entries – Anchor Butter is a current UK example. If you win, you'll find out either after the end of the draw window (eg. at the end of the hour), or after the final closing date of the promotion.

Winning packaging (instant win)

Occasionally the winning message is printed or enclosed in the packaging, in which case you need to keep the packaging to claim your prize. It might be a Gooless Creme Egg, a bag of blue sweets or a Willy Wonka-style golden ticket. Chances of winning a big prize this way are small. Companies might use 'reverse shoplifting' to put the winning packs in the shop – if you see someone doing this, watch carefully just in case they're planting the prize chocolate! If it's a promotion with thousands of winning products, see if you can spot subtle differences in product packaging when you scan the shelves – *Best Before* dates and batch codes may be printed differently on winning products.

Proof of purchase (receipt and/or packaging required)

Several years ago the UK law changed, and now it's okay to require a purchase for a random prize draw (you'll still see the 'no purchase necessary' route occasionally for Northern Ireland, where the laws are different). You sometimes need to post off your receipt, enter the details online or email a photo of it at the time of entry. I take a photo of the receipt on my phone as soon as I get home, save it with the product name in **Evernote**, then file the original away in my 'comps entered' box. Quite often if you win, you have to email a photo of your receipt rather than post it, so it saves scrabbling around in a panic, looking for the original if you get the call.

For some comps you keep the receipt and only post or email it if you're a winner – entry is usually via a simple text message or online. This type of promotion can be open to abuse, as there are a few people that enter purchase necessary competitions without a receipt. Just because you've heard a friend has won a prize in a POP competition, don't give up hope that *all* winners have been informed. The promoter may have asked for a receipt which the winner doesn't have – after waiting for a certain period of time (when the winner may cheekily be asking on comping forums for help!) they may invalidate that winner and draw again. Hold on to that proof of purchase for at least six months past the closing date, just in case. Unfortunately, for some promotions the receipt or POP is *never* asked for – so people *can* get away without buying the product.

Swipe to win/automatic entry

This is where you're entered into a prize draw when you buy a certain product and swipe your loyalty card (Nectar, Tesco, Superdrug, etc.) when you pay. It might also be hosted online, where purchase of a certain product automatically enters you into a prize draw. With these promotions, even people who don't want the prize and know nothing about the comp will be in the draw, so chances of winning are minimal – there's also the risk that a car will be awarded to someone without a driving licence, or an 18 year old student will win a family holiday for four! Just to prove that people *do* win 'swipe-to-win' comps though, a lucky Compers News member won a Vauxhall Adam car in last year's Tesco/Mars promotion.

44. Comp for charity

People always ask me if I buy lottery tickets. Of course I don't! It's a game of chance, with no way to improve my odds of winning apart from investing more money into tickets. I'd rather spend money on entering competitions, where my chance of a win is so much better. Although having said that, when it's a really enormous Euromillions jackpot, I do splash out on a few tickets and almost always win a small prize – I think we all love to dream of winning that HUGE cash prize don't we?

Raffles, on the other hand, are a different matter. I'm talking here about local fundraising raffles, or raffles that take place in a designated venue, where the number of entrants is minimal. I love a raffle, and if you've been lucky enough to attend any of the charity comping days I've helped to organise you'll understand why.

Well-organised raffles have the most incredible prizes, sometimes hundreds of them – and of course, every penny spent on tickets goes to charity. At our charity *Raising for Rainbows* comping days, some of our guests spent £50 on raffle tickets, and went home with prizes worth much, much more than that. You would be amazed at what companies are prepared to donate – expensive toiletries, holidays, jewellery, handbags, make-up, luxury food hampers etc.

There have been very few situations where I've not won a prize in a raffle – and that's because I'm generous with my spending. I tend not to donate to street collectors or sign up to give direct debits to charity. Instead, I prefer to spend enthusiastically at charity shops, events, raffles and tombolas, where I take along an empty sturdy bag and hope to take it home full of goodies! People sometimes hold back at a raffle for fear of appearing flashy, but I spend as much as I can afford. I don't feel guilty about buying ten times more tickets than anyone else – after all, it's for charity! And if even if you *don't* win, you've made a generous donation to a good cause. The most recent raffle I attended was in my local hall. I bought £40 of tickets and won two lovely prizes – a haircut in a city centre salon and Gold membership of Brighton Fringe festival, worth £75.

Always leave your raffle ticket buying until near the time of the draw, as you can usually get a good idea of how many people have entered and decide how many tickets to buy – be sure to watch the organisers put all your tickets into the draw! I spotted a beauty hamper raffle fundraising for *Tickled Pink* at a quiet Nottingham shopping centre. The raffle ticket book beside it only had 20 tickets sold, and it closed that afternoon. I bought ten tickets and won £100 of products.

Keep your raffle tickets somewhere safe – ideally in your hand. Sometimes there's no time for contact numbers to be scrawled on the back, so don't risk losing those winning numbers! Hang around until the winners are called – at some raffles, absent winners are assigned a random prize and other winners have a choice. If there's a tombola stall at the event you should check that out near the end – the organisers never want to take the prizes home again, so ticket price is usually dropped significantly.

You can also find charity prize draws or competitions online. Sometimes individuals (usually bloggers) ask for donations to a JustGiving fund in return for entry to win a prize. These don't usually get many entries. Use your Google and Twitter searching skills to find them, using phrases like *"donate and win"*, *"charity raffle"* or *"justgiving win"*. Despite being advertised nationwide, a *Tickled Pink* promotion at Asda a few years ago with a minimum online donation of £1 had almost as many prizes as entrants – I won a spa day for four people!

45. Make your tweets sweet

Twitter can seem confusing to a new user, but once you get the hang of it, you'll discover an amazing source of comps. The Twitter app is quick and easy to use on a mobile device, and even if you don't plan to use it much, it's worth joining Twitter for the comps with the big prizes, and to gain bonus entries in other prize draws.

Getting started is easy: go to **www.twitter.com**, and register with your name, email address, password, and choice of username. Add a profile photo, cover photo, location and biography to your Profile if you like – it's not essential but will help your account look more human.

How to enter Twitter comps

Before you start entering Twitter comps, I recommend you read my blog post and watch my video tutorial at **www.superlucky. me/EnterTwitterComps.**You can find lots of Twitter comps by following the search tips in the previous section. When you find a comp you want to enter, check if you need to follow the promoter – if you do, click *Follow* (or the silhouette icon with a plus sign). When you follow, you'll see that user's tweets on your *Home* news feed.

Most Twitter giveaways involve a *Retweet* or *RT* – sharing the tweet to your own *timeline* so your followers can see it. To retweet, look underneath a tweet for the double arrow *Retweet* icon and tap or click it. It's absolutely fine to retweet someone else's competition retweet (in the past this wasn't the case!), as the promoter won't know it came via someone else. The comper *will* be notified though, so only do it if you're happy for that person to know you're copying their entries. If you'd rather not retweet other people's entries, then right-click or ctrl-click the 'timestamp' on the tweet (eg. *35m* or *2h*) to open the original in a new tab, and retweet directly from the promoter's original tweet.

You may be asked to *Favourite* or *Star* a tweet – just tap the star underneath to do this. For some tweets, you'll be asked to *Reply* with an answer, photo or link – perhaps including a hashtag (this is sometimes referred to as a *Comment*, as your tweet will appear under the original tweet). To reply, tap the single arrow under a tweet. The promoter's username will automatically be *tagged* at the start of your reply – along with anyone else mentioned, or the person who retweeted that tweet. It's a good idea to delete those extra name tags, just leaving the promoter's name.

Most Twitter promotions are *RT and Follow* prize draws, which are popular and easy to enter. If you only enter this kind of promotion, your timeline will be nothing but retweets and Twitter will start to filter your tweets out of searches believing you're a spammer or a 'bot'. To avoid this, you should add original content to your

Twitter feed by tweeting your own messages, and replying to other users. Get into the habit of sending out random tweets. It will feel unnatural and silly at first but *'Happy Monday everyone!'*, *'Gorgeous sunset in Brighton tonight'* and the like will make your account look genuine rather than a big list of retweeted content. If you can make a few Twitter friends and have a conversation with them, even better – you could start by tweeting me at @ superluckydi!

You can also choose to *Quote Tweet* rather than Retweet, which means you add your own comment or text when you share the promoter's tweet. It's not clear whether this will be classed as a retweet by the promoter, so it's probably only worth doing for 'reply' type competitions.

Twitter tips

- Retweet near the closing time if possible.

- Interact with and reply to other tweets – if your timeline is full of retweets and little else, Twitter may think you're a spam account, filtering your tweets from searches.

- RTs are easy to do on your phone when you're out and about, but don't focus all your attention on them – try creative Twitter comps too.

- If the promoter sends out several competition tweets, RT all of them to increase your chance of a win – they are likely to choose a winner from just one of those tweets.

- Copy and paste the competition hashtag into your tweet – if you spell it wrong, your entry won't be seen.

- If you want to retweet directly from a Twitter list, that's fine as long as the tweet shows the promoter's icon and *'<username> retweeted'* above it. The tweeter will be notified of your retweet, so only do it if you're happy for them to know you're copying them.

- Advanced users can use **Tweetdeck** (tip 73) or **Hootsuite** to manage multiple Twitter columns – set up a column searching for 'RT win' which will constantly update with new content.

If you have time, send a reply as well as a retweet. It's expensive for the software to choose a random winner fairly for a RT giveaway and in many cases the promoter will be choosing from a list of replies or recent entries instead.

Hitting your limits

The main problem for compers is that you can only follow 2,000 users on Twitter. After this point, there are limits to the number of additional users you can follow based on your ratio of followers to following – you will have to get about 1,800 followers in order to start following new accounts. It's very hard to get to that number unless you blog, run giveaways or get involved in a lot of chat online. When you reach your 2,000 limit, use a tool like Manageflitter to clean up your account. Log in to your Twitter account at **www.manageflitter.com**, and you'll see who you're following and how active they are on Twitter. Remove dormant accounts or accounts which haven't been used for a few months or so – you'd be surprised how many company Twitter accounts are abandoned. To reduce numbers further, don't follow your comping mates on Twitter – put them into a Twitter list and view that separately as a source of comps.

46. Go to Twitter parties

Twitter parties are becoming more popular as a fun way for people to *live chat*, using a unique hashtag. They are scheduled at a set time, usually for an hour, and are often combined with an opportunity to win prizes. A particularly successful Twitter party will result in the hashtag appearing in 'trending' lists, which is great for the promoter. Twitter parties are fast-moving and frantic, so it can be a bit wild if you drop in on one.

At the moment most parties are hosted in US but there are several hosted in the UK, with a good chance of winning a prize if you take part. I share details of Twitter parties on the SuperLucky Facebook page or simply search for 'win Twitter party' to find them.

Hosts

There will be one or more party hosts who will keep the chat going by sharing tips or asking questions – the main host may be the sponsor, or they might use a social media influencer to take charge, for example @BritMums or a popular blogger. For a party with prizes, you will normally have to follow the host(s) to be eligible for a prize. Spot prizes may be awarded and announced during the party, or all participants may be entered into a draw at the end of the party.

Hashtags

A Twitter party uses a unique hashtag (#), and Twitter search is used to keep track of all the tweets sent with that hashtag. Promoters should choose their hashtags carefully – a party thrown to celebrate Susan Boyle's new album with the hashtag #susanalbumparty was a PR nightmare!

How to join a Twitter party

- Follow the party host(s) and sponsor(s)

- When the party has started, search Twitter for the party hashtag, and click *Live* to see the most recent results

- Reply to questions that the host asks, using the party hashtag. Upper and lower case doesn't matter with hashtags, but you might want to copy the sponsor's hashtag exactly.

There are several methods you can use to keep track of tweets during a party. Here are a few:

- Using **www.twitter.com**, you'll need a browser window open with the sponsor's tweets, plus a second browser window open for the hashtag search.

- At **www.twubs.com** log in with your Twitter details, then enter the party hashtag. You'll get a live stream, where you reply and retweet by hovering to the right of the tweet – when you hit reply, the tweet is shown below the blank box at the top so you can see what question you're answering. The hashtag is added automatically to your tweets.

- **www.tweetdeck.com** uses streaming columns to keep track of Twitter activity, so is great for compers to add specific search columns. Click the + sign to add two new columns to your Tweetdeck, a User column (input the host name) and a Search column (input the hashtag). Read more about Tweetdeck in the **Tools of the Trade** section.

"I joined a BritMums Twitter party thanks to a post on the SuperLucky Facebook page and couldn't believe it when I won the the top prize of a Kenwood Chef mixer worth £300. I'd never heard of Twitter parties until I read about them on SuperLucky. I've won at three out of the four parties that I've participated in so far and the prizes of supermarket vouchers come in very handy indeed!"– *Joanna Krakowiak*

---

47. Take lots of photos

Don't be scared of photo competitions. 'Effort' competitions give you the best chance of winning – and in some cases there are fewer entries than prizes. More and more promoters are opting to reward random winners with prizes rather than judging all the entries, which means that anyone can have a go regardless of the quality of their photography. If you have a smartphone, use that rather than a digital camera for photos to enter in social media competitions – they will only be viewed at a small size.

I've won a lot of prizes in fun photo comps – my first was in 1998 when I posted off a selfie (it was a 6 x 4 print back in those days!) to Minx magazine and won a trip to Reykjavik. My most recent photo wins are £1,000 of Selfridges vouchers, a trip to Legoland Denmark and flights to New York – all from Instagram competitions. One of my top tips is to try selfie competitions – many compers hate to show their face, so that means selfie comps are very low entry. Read more tips in the **Love your selfie** section (tip 63).

Before you enter a photo competition, read the T&Cs carefully. Some promoters may take ownership of entries (winning or not) and use them for advertising and marketing – with no payment or credit to you. In most cases, they're not that sneaky, and will only want to share your entry in conjunction with promoting the competition. Make sure you check the T&Cs and are happy about this before entering! For some competitions, you won't be able to enter a photo that has already been entered into another competition – this is the reason I recommend taking a lot of similar photographs, rather than just one.

Photography tips

- Try to take your photos with natural lighting. Go near windows or doors when taking photos indoors, and to sources of light like neon signs or street lamps when outdoors. Avoid back light when taking pictures of people (unless you want a silhouette).

- Try to picture the result you want in your head – draw it if you can!

- Take photos at unusual angles.

- Consider the background of your photo – patterned wallpaper may look better than an untidy bookshelf.

- Make sure you include all the important things in the shot – you can always crop it later on.

- Take the photo on a normal setting, and add filters later.

- Use the burst setting (hold your finger down on an iPhone) to get lots of quick photos of an action shot – then choose the best one.

- Give your camera lens a regular clean.

- Take plenty of snaps of your children or pets – lots of magazines want these on their letters pages.

- Take lots of photos of the same scene, so you can enter them in separate comps.

- If you're taking a photo featuring a product, also take it without the product.

- Invest in accessories like a small tripod, a remote control button, selfie stick or special lenses.

Smartphone tips

- Use the back camera as much as possible – the front-facing camera has a lower resolution.

- Use the volume button on the side of an iPhone to take a photo – sometimes it's easier than tapping the screen.

- Tap on the screen to focus.

- Tap on a dark area of the screen to lighten the photo.

- Pinch your fingers in and out to zoom.

- Use the self-timer – if you don't have one in your camera app, try *TimerCam*.

- Use an app like Photogrid - or the built in 'Layout' option in Instagram – to make collages. These often stand out amongst other entries.

- Photograph old prints and add Instagram filters to them.

You'll probably end up with quite a lot of random photos saved on various devices. To keep them safe in one place consider using cloud storage or something like Dropbox or Drive (tip 77). Every so often, go through and resave them with a relevant file name (or tag). In my Dropbox I have a variety of themed folders: Christmas, kids, travel, food, hair, fashion, etc.

"When I could no longer use a laptop or PC properly because of an accident, hubby bought me an iPad so I could carry on my comping. It's been my lifeline as I can operate it with my one properly functioning little finger. Since I started reading SuperLucky I've had the courage to enter photo competitions. I have a small camera that I can balance on my hands and press the button with my little finger. Because I have to take my time, I look more at what I am doing. A few weeks ago I had my first photo win with a shot I had taken of a bee – I won a canvas Wanderlust bag with some lovely books!" – Kaz Bridges

---

48. Enter Instagram competitions

Instagram is a free app for mobile devices, designed for people to share original, creative photos with their friends and followers. Take a picture or video with your mobile device, choose a filter to transform it, then share to Instagram – you can also choose to share to Facebook or Twitter. Instagram does a fabulous job of making mediocre photos look magical.

If you're new to Instagram, the best place to get started is on the Help Pages at **www.instagram.com**, which will guide you through setting up your account and profile, home screen options, taking, sharing and editing photos and more. You can view, like and comment on Instagram photos on a computer at www.instagram.com, but the only way to upload photos is to use a mobile device unless you install the *Bluestacks* app.

Instagram is a great platform for promoters to host creative, fun competitions. Lots of brands get Instagram promotions right – they encourage entrants to create something new and visually interesting and share it with a hashtag or two. Some promoters simply ask for a Like or a Comment on their photo as an entry, and others ask you to *regram* their photo on your own timeline.

Before you start entering Instagram competitions, take a look at my blog post and video tutorial at **www.superlucky.me/ EnterInstagramComps**.

How to upload a photo for an Instagram competition

- Before entering, carefully check the competition details – read the T&Cs to see if it's random or judged, and how many entries you can make. T&Cs will often be linked in the promoter's biography, as you can't make clickable links in Instagram comments.

- Write down the hashtag and any @ tags/mentions you need to use in your caption – or have the instructions in front of you on a computer.

- Take a photo by tapping the Instagram camera icon, or navigate to your camera roll to choose an existing photo.

- Edit your photo by tapping the spanner icon – crop it, rotate it and change all sorts of settings.

- Tap the filter icon on the left to add effects – you can change the impact of these by tapping the filter again and using a slider.

- Tap Next and add a caption, tagging the company and using a competition hashtag if required.

- Share your photo to Instagram.

- If you've included a competition hashtag, tap it to check that your entry appears on search results. If not, delete and re-upload. Don't use any other hashtags in addition to the specified one – there are a few 'broken' hashtags that may stop your entry showing in search results (for example, #photography, #instagram and #love may all cause problems).

If you're going to enter lots of Instagram comps, always set your phone camera to the square setting.

49. Learn to regram

Instagram likes original content, so regramming, reposting or sharing a post isn't a built-in function of the app. That means these types of prize draws are usually low entry – mainly because people don't know *how* to regram, or don't *like* to regram! A regram is a bit like a Facebook share or a Twitter RT, but trickier to do.

There are a few ways to regram – I use a screenshot because it's quick to do on an iPhone. Dependent on your device, you might find it easier to use an app – I have a guide and video tutorial for both methods at **www.superlucky.me/RegramGuide**.

Regram using a screenshot

- First, follow the promoter on Instagram – this may not be compulsory, but it's good manners.

- With the promoter's competition photo on your screen, take a screenshot. On an iPhone or iPad hold down the *Home* button and then press the *Power* button. On an Android it's usually the *Power* and *Volume Down* buttons together – for other devices, you might need to Google to find out what method to use.

- A photo of the screen will now be saved on your camera roll or gallery.

- Click the camera icon on Instagram, tap on the left of the screen to access your photo gallery and select your screenshot.

- Move the image with your finger to crop it, removing the surrounding white and text so it looks like the original shot.

- Tap *Next* twice, skipping the filters.

- Add a caption with the competition hashtag (if there is one) and tag the promoter – the tag might not be compulsory but it lets them know you've entered, so I prefer to include it.

- Finally, tap the competition hashtag (if there is one) and check that your photo appears on the search results page.

Regram using the Regram app

There are several regramming apps available including Photo Repost, and Repostapp – the instructions here are for **Regram**.

- In Instagram, tap the heart on the competition photo to add it to your Likes.

- Open your regram app and tap *Likes*.

- Find the competition photo, and tap the *Regram* button.

- Choose an option for the overlay bar – this displays the original user's name.

- Tap *Instagram* to open the photo in Instagram.

- Tap *Next*.

- Delete all text except the relevant hashtag and @ tags – you might want to add your own caption. If you want to make it clear it's a repost rather than your own photo, use the #regram hashtag, or use 'RG' or #repost at the start of your caption.

- Share.

- You might want to like and comment on the original photo to say you've entered, just like people do on Facebook.

Keep in mind that Regrams are usually ugly text-heavy photos, so it's best not to share lots of them at once – similar to Facebook 'Like

& Share' comps, regrams make your profile look a bit 'comper' and spammy. Mix them up with your own original shots.

> *"I entered a regram competition after seeing it on SuperLucky and was amazed and delighted to win a Citröen! We'd been thinking of buying a second car and winning a car was top of my wishlist!"* – Sandra Bald

50. Cook up a prize

We all have to eat, so why not make your meal a competition entry too? If you cook something that looks good, snap a quick photo on your phone before you tuck in – you never know when it might come in handy. In summer, take photos of family picnics and barbecues outside – these are a common theme for photo competitions.

To take a good photo of a meal, hold your cameraphone horizontally above the table, plate or pan, and take a square photo. Do this with as much natural light as possible. For inspiration check out some of the top food bloggers' Instagram accounts – look at **@ deliciouslyella**, **@amummytoo** and my local Brighton friend **@ kitsunetsukiki** for mouthwateringly beautiful photos.

If you're taking a photo for a specific competition, take a few different shots of the meal in a couple of settings. Make sure you're in one of them, to prove you made it yourself – get someone to take a photo of you tucking in to your handiwork! If you don't win that specific competition, there are plenty of magazines who print readers' recipes in return for a prize – my Halloween eyeball soup (featuring carved radishes!) won me several prizes and was printed in a recipe magazine.

If you're not much good at cooking, don't let that put you off – a surprising number of photo promotions are actually random prize draws, so everyone has a chance of winning no matter how their photo looks.

For some competitions, you might be asked to create a recipe using a certain product – popcorn, tortilla wraps, peanut butter, Marmite, etc. Searching Google and Pinterest will give you inspiration and show you what looks good in a photo. Take photos of your creation with and without the product packaging, and see what looks best.

It can be good fun to get the kids involved with food comps – pizza and cupcake decorating is a great after school activity. If they make a mess in the kitchen, take a photo of that too – Ryland's messy muffins moment, covered in flour and chocolate, is one of my favourite competition winners!

"For a Lindeman's competition, I cooked three dishes for a spring menu. I used Lindeman's wine in all three dishes and it was the overall winner – I won a £250 supermarket voucher and three cases of wine!" – Rebecca B

---

51. Be a movie maker

Video competitions get very few entries. Shooting, editing and uploading a video might seem a daunting prospect for most compers, but with the latest smartphones, tablets and apps it's actually a simple task. Making a short movie is fun, and if you have family or friends who can help out then you could be on to a winner.

If you use a digital camera or video camera, you'll need to connect it by cable to your computer to upload footage. On a PC, *Windows Movie Maker* enables you to edit and add titles, transitions, effects, music, and more. On a Mac, *iMovie* is the best software for editing. There are helpful guides online to using **Movie Maker** and **iMovie** at **http://bit.ly/WinMoviMaker** and **http://bit.ly/iMovieHlp.**

With a smartphone or tablet you can easily create short films, and share them quickly to YouTube, Vimeo, Instagram, Twitter or Vine. Beware that videos will take up lots of memory on your phone so you might want to back them up to a computer or to *cloud* storage online.

Recording footage on your cameraphone

- Recording video is as easy as opening up your camera app and tapping a video icon, or swiping from photo to video setting on an iPhone or iPad.

- Tap the red button to start recording, then tap again to stop recording. The film will be saved to your camera roll.

- Record with your phone held landscape rather than portrait – it will be bigger and better when it's shared on YouTube, a website or a Facebook page.

- On an iPhone or iPad, pinch your fingers together to zoom in and out whilst recording.

- On an iPhone use Slo-Mo or Time-Lapse effects – swipe to the left past Video to try these out.

- If you want to trim your film on an iPhone, tap on it and then tap on the edges of the film strip on the screen, moving the markers to shorten it to the length you require.

- If you want to edit clips together on a phone, you'll need an app – *VidTrim* for Android or *Splice* for iPhone/iPad are both available as free versions, and Apple's *iMovie* is excellent if you want to buy an app.

- Once you have finished your film, send it by email, share to Twitter, post to Facebook, or upload to YouTube/Vimeo directly from your device.

Vine

Vine is a free app for tablets and smartphones which lets users create and share looping video clips up to a maximum of six seconds long. It's used successfully for short funnies and clever stop-motion films, and is a fun and easy way to practise making videos. Download Vine at **http://vine.co/** and register with your Twitter account or email address.

To start recording, tap the camera icon. Holding your finger on the screen starts filming, and releasing your finger pauses it. Your Vine can be between three and six seconds long, and be a single shot or several small clips put together. After recording, you can edit your clips – when you've finished editing, tap *Save*, add a caption and share. You can also send your video to Twitter or Facebook – connect the accounts by going to your Profile page and updating your settings.

To find the URL (web address) for your Vine, tap the upward arrow under it, then tap the three dots at the top of the screen and choose *copy* – the link will be copied to the clipboard.

Vine can be tricky to master because to create a successful Vine, the looping should work smoothly with sound and visuals. You might want to browse a few top rated Vines to see what looks good!

Instagram

Instagram is mainly used to share photos, but it's possible to share between 3 and 15 seconds of video in a similar way to Vine. With Instagram, you can easily add effects to films. Download Instagram at **www.instagram.com** and sign up with your email, username and a password.

- To record video, tap the camera icon at the bottom of the app, then change to the video icon.

- Hold your finger on the button to start recording, and release your finger to stop.

- Tap *Next* to add an optional filter, choose a cover frame or mute your clip.

- Tap *Next* – on the *Share* screen add a caption, tag the promoter, include a hashtag or add a location before posting to your profile.

- Send your video to Twitter or Facebook by tapping the icons before sharing.

If you want to share an existing video clip recorded with your phone camera, simply tap the bottom right icon to go to your phone's video album, choose a video, and tap *Next*. Trim it by tapping the scissors icon and moving your fingers on the video strip at the bottom to choose the start and end points. Add filters and share as above.

Tips

- Plan your film on paper before you start recording.

- Use a tripod – a Gorillapod is easy to pop into your bag and great for phones.

- Ensure you have a good light source, and don't film when it's too windy as the noise will be off-putting.

- Check the rules carefully before you start – some promoters won't allow under 18s, copyrighted music or brand names in the video.

- Search on the competition hashtag first to see what you're up against and check your fabulous original idea hasn't already been used.

- If you're automatically sharing to Twitter from Vine or Instagram, check your caption isn't too long (the hashtag might be cut from the tweet) – it's safer to copy the link to your entry then compose a new tweet with that link at the end.

- If the promoter asks for a photo *or* video entry, opt for a video – your entry is sure to stand out.

- Consider making a short film even when the promoter doesn't ask for one – a fun video rather than a Facebook comment or a tweeted photo can really stand out amongst other entries in a judged competition, particularly if it incorporates the product or brand.

- Hold your phone or tablet landscape to fit more in. If it needs to be uploaded to Vine or Instagram it will be cropped to a square, so keep the important action in the centre of the shot.

"I watched Di's Ocado video entry a year or so ago and it gave me the encouragement to make our own videos – having teenagers in the house to help with the techie stuff helps as well. I have won two lots of sponsorship for my son's football team totalling £5,000 using the same video and I also won a trip to Florida with Virgin holidays!" –
Laura Bryant

---

52. Try Gleam and Rafflecopter giveaways

Gleam and Rafflecopter are giveaway 'widgets' that are embedded on blogs, Facebook pages and websites, and can be a little bewildering. More promoters have started to use them to give away big prizes like games consoles and holidays though, so it's worth learning how to use them. Find UK Gleam and Rafflecopter giveaways listed at **www.superlucky.me/linky**, by following blogs – or simply searching Google.

Promoters and bloggers like using Rafflecopter and Gleam because the basic plans are free, flexible and offer an easy way to administer prize draws. Entries are tracked and a random winner is chosen fairly and can be displayed on the widget. The widgets also capture email addresses, so winners can be contacted directly (the email address they have access to depends on whether you logged in to the widget using Facebook, Twitter or email). Promoters can choose what to display at the top of the widget – usually you will see a countdown to the closing date, the total entries in the draw and the number of entries you have in the draw. Underneath this is the prize, then a list of entry tasks. Never let a large number of entries or tasks put you off – depending on how the widget is set up, in some cases you can earn 100+ entries. However, it usually only takes the completion of one task to get your name in the draw.

Entry via Gleam is much less fiddly than Rafflecopter as, once you've logged in, it's single click entry for many tasks. Rafflecopter, on the other hand, can involve a lot of copying, pasting and typing into the widget. Once you've logged into Gleam or Rafflecopter it should remember you, so you don't need to log in for each new giveaway.

Tasks

You rarely have to do all the tasks listed – usually they are all optional, and completing just one will get you an entry in the prize draw. If that's not the case, and there are mandatory entries, that *should* be mentioned in the accompanying text. Sometimes completing the first few tasks will unlock other optional tasks – do as few or as many tasks as you choose.

- **Answer a question.** You'll usually need to leave your answer in the widget – this may involve visiting the sponsor's website to choose a favourite product or find the answer.

- **Comment on the blog post.** Scroll down and look for *leave a comment* or *leave a reply* – you may need to click on the word *Comments* or a speech bubble icon for the comments to show. Some blogs use Facebook comments, for others you might need to use Google, Wordpress or Disqus to log in. Type your comment into the empty box, with an email address if required (this won't be published). If there's an option to leave a website address, leave it blank – this is for bloggers to leave their blog link. Some blogs moderate comments so yours may not appear immediately. Remember, all Rafflecopter and Gleam giveaways are random prize draws, not judged competitions – but you still need to ensure your comment answers the question and is a valid entry.

- **Visit on Facebook.** Visit a Facebook page – you don't need to Like it.

- **Follow on Twitter.**

- **Tweet.** With Gleam, hover over the word *tweet* to view the text you'll be tweeting, then click to tweet. It's more complicated with Rafflecopter: a window will open where you can view the tweet text and after tweeting you need to find and copy the URL of the tweet to paste into the widget.

- **Follow on Pinterest/Instagram.** There's usually a clickable link to a profile page, where you can click *Follow*.

- **Subscribe to a YouTube channel.** Click the *Subscribe* button, and YouTube will open in another window. If you're logged in, click *Subscribe*, close the window and click *Done*, or *Continue*.

- **Subscribe to a blog or newsletter.** This could be automatic when you click, or there may be instructions on how to subscribe.

- **Refer friends for extra entries.** You're given a unique link to share on social media or via email. For every one of your friends who enters the giveaway via your link, you get a bonus entry.

- **Bonus entry.** This is to encourage you to revisit the blog, click it daily for a bonus entry.

Tips

- **Use browser bookmarks** to save favourite giveaways into a daily folder – daily tweets or sharing referral links can give you lots of extra entries and increase your chance of winning considerably. For example, a giveaway on a parenting blog might have 120 entries, from 30 people completing 4 tasks each. If you do the 4 tasks, but also tweet daily for 8 days, you'll have 12 entries in the draw compared to everyone else's 4 entries - you've increased your chance of winning from 1-in-30 to 1-in-10.

- If the widget doesn't display, refresh the page.

- In some cases, the widget won't display on a blog post and you'll have to click a line of text – eg. *'a Rafflecopter giveaway'* – which will take you to the Rafflecopter site. This is because free Wordpress sites don't allow Javascript.

If you want to start using Rafflecopter and Gleam, I recommend you spend time looking at my two video guides: **www.superlucky. me/RafflecopterGuide** and **www.superlucky.me/GleamGuide**.

"Most of my wins are from blogs using Gleam and Rafflecopter. My biggest Rafflecopter win was a limited edition Maclaren Volo Dylan's Candy Bar buggy. My advice is to look for the low entry ones, but if the prize is something you really want then go for it, no matter how many have entered already. You have to be in it to win it!"
– Helen Grounds

---

53. Pin to win

Pinterest is one of my favourite ways to enter a competition – it's creative and inspiring, and promoters are enjoying it too. I've won some lovely prizes on Pinterest, including a year's supply of kids shoes from Cloggs, £500 of blinds from Hillary's and £1,000 of Harveys Furniture. It can be time-consuming – but if you enjoy beautiful photography and have an eye for colour and design, it's a nice change from form-filling. Even if you don't consider yourself creative, entry to some Pinterest prize draws is as simple as re-pinning an image – so you can still have a go.

With Pinterest you create online themed *boards*, which you fill with individual *pins* (photos or videos). It's a visual way of bookmarking things you like, for example destinations, recipes, crafts or products. With most *pins*, you click them to go to the original image or video on a website – it might show you details of how to cook a recipe, or to buy a dress in an online shop. Amongst the *pins* you'll also find infographics: long, tall images with lots of useful information.

To join Pinterest, simply head to **www.pinterest.com**. You'll have the option to link your Facebook or Twitter account, or join with just your email address. Try to stick with a consistent username if you already have a Twitter or Instagram account, and use the same profile photo, so people know it's you. Once your account is active, check your settings to adjust the amount of email notifications you get.

Before you start entering Pinterest comps, take a look at my blog post and video tutorial, which you can find at **www.superlucky. me/PinToWin**. This will show you how to get started and give you plenty of tips.

The main types of prize promotion on Pinterest are re-pinning existing pins, or creating a complete new board. For a re-pin, the winner is chosen at random, and for a board the winner can be chosen at random or by judges. Deciding a winner based on the number of Likes, Followers or Re-pins is, thankfully, rare.

To enter a re-pin prize draw/sweepstakes

- You'll usually have to follow the promoter – click *Follow* on their profile page. Like Twitter or Instagram, following someone means you see their posts on your *Home* page.

- Find the competiton photo you need to pin, and click *Pin it* at the top.

- Select or create a *Board* to pin your photo to.

- Click *See it now* to open up your new pin, and copy a link to it from your browser address bar (on the Pinterest app, click the triple dot menu and select *Copy Link*).

- Depending on the instructions, you may need to comment on the original post with your link, tweet it to the promoter or paste it into an entry form.

To create a board for a competition

- Click *Create board* on your profile page, and name it according to the competition rules – add a description, including any specified hashtag.

- Add pins to your board from a Pinterest keyword search, a Google search, favourite websites, or even upload your own photos (watch my video guide at **http://superlucky.me/ PinToWin** for how to do this).

- On a board, pins will display with the oldest at the bottom and the most recent at the top, and you can't rearrange them. If you want your board to look good, plan the content in advance before pinning.

- Add descriptions or hashtags to the photos if required, but keep in mind most promoters won't have time to read the text – first impressions count.

- Copy the link to your board from your browser address bar – you'll usually have to paste this link as a comment on the original competition post, although you may be asked to tweet it or share on Facebook.

Pinterest Tips

- Sticking to a set colour theme can be very effective, or graduating from one colour to another with your pins (this will have to be carefully planned!).

- Beautiful type and words amongst your photos will help your entry stand out.

- If you're looking for pins for a competition board, don't re-pin from another board that somebody has created for the same competition – it's bad manners! If you really want to use that particular photo, trace it back to its original website by clicking on it, or to its original board by clicking underneath the pin – then pin from there.

- Check the boards of other entrants to see what they've been pinning – you don't really want to feature the same pins that they have.

- If you're re-pinning from elsewhere on Pinterest, click the photo first to ensure it doesn't take you to a spam website. Some spammers will repin a popular photo and then update the linked URL to something completely different.

- Don't pin photos that are too small – they look awful when you click them for a closer look. Want to find a bigger version? Right-click or ctrl-click and choose *Search Google for this image* from the drop down menu, to see if a larger version exists online.

- Choose tall (portrait) photos where possible. They appear bigger and have more impact than wide (landscape) images.

- If you find a really great photo, click to view it and scroll down below it to see *Also on these boards* and *Related Pins* – clicking through these can result in some rare and amazing finds – and also keep you engrossed for hours.

"Some of my best wins have come from Pinterest. I really enjoy the creative process of putting a board together and it's well worth spending a good couple of hours on a competition entry to bag that amazing prize!" –
Joanna Krakowiak

Tips for winning competitions

So, you're up and running with comping. You're finding great competitions and prize draws, and entering them correctly. But how can you give yourself the very best chance of actually *winning* a prize? This section will give you the tips you need to start winning regularly.

54. Get your family and friends on board

If you can encourage your family and friends to support this new hobby, you'll win a lot more prizes. When you start comping, your friends will think you're the biggest weirdo around. In all honesty this opinion probably won't change, you just need to ensure they find this habit of yours fun and quirky rather than irritating – make sure you #embraceyourweird. Keep them sweet by sharing prizes with them; when my friends pop over I send them home with Lambrini, chocolate and lipsticks!

I'm often approached by compers who tell me they keep their hobby quiet because their husband doesn't approve, or their kids are embarrassed. If this is an issue then the best way to change their opinion is to win them something fabulous. Consider what prizes your husband or kids would love, perhaps a driving experience at a race track or a day out at Legoland. Think on a smaller scale too. A treatment at a beauty salon, or tickets to see your favourite football team are both little treats. Sporty prizes get *very* low entry numbers – mainly because the majority of compers are female, and not sports fans. Local radio stations and newspapers often give away tickets to football matches. A few years back I won tickets for four of us to go to a Championship game of my choice and present the Man of the Match award. I took Rob and two of his (Forest-supporting) friends to see Nottingham Forest beat Derby County – his mates didn't take the mickey out of my hobby after that!

Add your family's prize ideas to your wishlist and make sure you're regularly Googling for competitions to win them. Winning something like football or cinema tickets can have a hidden bonus for you too – the chance of a few hours of quiet comping while the family enjoy your latest prize!

If you have children, be sure to enter kids' competitions. My son Ryland isn't exceptionally artistic but occasionally his drawing has been the *only* entry in a competition, so he's won the prize. The look of delight on his face when he gets a parcel from the postman is priceless – watch Ry opening some of his goodies in my Prize Unboxing videos at **www.youtube.com/superluckydi**.

If you have the support of your family you'll be able to relax and enjoy comping more – and if you can train them to pick up entry forms and free magazines, you'll be laughing!

"I am a naturally mad and embarrassing person (or so my kids tell me) so am always happy to go that extra mile and use my sense of humour to catch the judge's eye. My eldest daughter is due to head off to university so it has become the family's mission to all comp together to win her some nice stuff for her to leave home with! Di's advice to involve the whole family has given us much fun and prizes!" –
Fiona Haward

---

55. Work as a team

Many compers work alone, but it pays to get organised and have friends to call upon in certain situations. Setting up a secret Facebook group to share ideas with your closest comping mates is a great idea – but make sure you trust each other! Here are a few suggestions on working together:

- Team up for 'purchase necessary' competitions which have a single prize. The group share the cost of the product, keep the receipt and it's agreed if one of the group wins, they get the receipt to claim the prize.

- Help out for a radio quiz. This is great if you have local friends who are regularly online. You can all call up for the same on-air radio competition, and be online in a Facebook chat discussing the answers. My friend Vic tuned in to the radio to identify a song clip for me, helping me to win £1,000!

- If you have to submit photos of a hard-to-find product, shop window display or a specific London taxi, take plenty of photos with different angles and send the photos to your mates so they can enter too.

- There are sometimes tricky picture quizzes online and in magazines, with clues so hard you could never get them all yourself. Working as a team to get the answers is a great idea – but it's better to do it in a secret group or private forum, rather than an open forum where anyone can copy your answers.

- If you have a friend who enjoys creative competitions, brainstorm ideas and work on the projects together – it's always better to embarrass yourself with a mate. You'll get two entries instead of one, and can share the prize if one of you wins – or even go on the prize holiday together!

"I won a holiday to Oz thanks to Di and other friends on Instant Messenger. I decided to ring a radio station on the Thursday morning, answered a question and the following day I had to go head-to-head against another lady. I arranged for Di and my friends to be online the next morning to help out. All the questions were based on Australia and my quick-fingered friends found the answers for me. Six questions later I had won my dream holiday to Australia!" – Marie Lomax

---

56. Make your entry stand out

It's important to focus on those wishlist prizes – if you *really* want the prize, you must let the promoter know. Making my entries stand out was how I racked up dozens of major prizes in supposedly 'random' draws in the nineties and noughties. These days I prefer to use my talents in judged competitions, but there are a few tricks I still use to make an impression in a prize draw. Despite the efforts of CAP and the ASA, many promoters *don't* choose their random prize draw winners fairly under independent supervision – meaning that clever compers can use eyecatching tricks to increase their chances of getting picked.

Back in the late 90s and early 2000s I created huge, bright homemade postcards to send off – Royal Mail hate it of course, but I've had success with cards shaped like Christmas stockings, handbags and skulls. My favourite was a big alien head covered with sparkly green foam, which won me a wonderful break in Prague with GAME. Fun postcards also won me trips to Tokyo and Spain – and after sharing my tips in the office, a friend went on to win a family trip to Florida with a huge homemade dolphin postcard!

Back in 2008, after two amazing adventures in Japan and South America, Rob asked, "Do you think we could do something a bit more relaxing for our next trip – how about a week's holiday on a beach?" Finding that prize wasn't as hard as I thought – I spotted a magazine with an entry form competition to win a week's holiday at Sandals in the Caribbean. Perfect! But this time I decided to do more than send off one of my homemade postcards. I'd spotted something on eBay that was ideal – a 'beach-in-a-box' featuring sand, a mini deckchair, parasol and beach ball. I'd noticed the entries were going directly to the Marketing Department of the magazine and thought they might be impressed with something a little bit quirky. It was a risk of course – they might (and should!) have conducted a proper supervised random draw from all the entries. But for a few quid I decided it was worth a try. I attached my entry form to the 'beach-in-a-box' and posted it Recorded Delivery to arrive on the closing date. The following week I received a phone call from the Marketing Department telling me how excited they were to receive my entry, and that I was the winner. Keep in mind this technique won't work with every address – the big handling houses that use PO Box addresses should *always* be choosing winners at random under independent supervision, whereas entries sent directly to a company's Marketing Department will have a better chance of being picked.

If you're sending off an entry form, rather than put it in an envelope, glue it to the back of a homemade postcard – or stick it inside a folded sheet of card, then fold it in half and secure with a bit of fancy tape. Ryland and I created a Lego head from yellow cardboard last year, stuck the entry form inside it and won an annual Legoland pass.

Some people might consider this 'cheating' – but my entries are still being sent on a postcard or entry form as specified in the rules. I'm just adding a little something extra to make them stand out! Many promoters *don't* select winners under independent supervision, and I recommend compers should take full advantage of that where possible.

Though these entry methods might be tricky to apply in their original postal format now, they can definitely be successful when adapted to work on social media too. Here are some easy ways to make your entry stand out:

- Make *yourself* stand out. Choose a good avatar, fun screen name and entertaining biography.

- Liven up Facebook comments with jokes, poems, stories, emojis and photos. On a Facebook post, photo comments are more likely to get a Like and the most popular comments will be pushed to the top of the comments list, so the promoter will see them first. Imagine a promoter scrolling through 4,000 comments – most will get bored after a few screens of names, so you need to get your entry near the top of the list if you can!

- If the rules don't state a limit, enter multiple times.

- Record your poem or slogan entry on Vine or Instagram as a video.

- For a photo competition, combine multiple photos using an app like *Photogrid* (see my Photogrid tutorial **at www.superlucky. me/2014/09/using-photogrid**) or the built in Layout feature on Instagram.

- Decorate your postal entries, or send objects.

- For your comments and tweets, be relevant, positive and funny, using unusual words or writing styles.

Promotions advertised as 'judged' sometimes end up as a random draw – and there are many occasions when people have been rather surprised by the high quality of an entry apparently chosen at 'random' too! Until the ASA make more effort to educate promoters and agencies about following the CAP Code, I recommend you *always* do your best to make your entry stand out.

"It's hard not to be inspired by Di's enthusiasm for comping, so when I saw a prize draw to 'Win a Cherokee Jeep' I decided to give it a go. Remembering Di's advice to make your entry stand out from all the others, I sent my details in with a toy Jeep. When I received a letter telling me I had won the prize draw, I was amazed and absolutely over the moon. It was perfect timing as I was about to buy my first house. I sold the Jeep and used half the money as a deposit for my mortgage and the other half to buy a new car!" – Emma Thornhill

---

57. Share the love

Now, this tip could be confusing when later on I'm urging you to keep a secret! But to maximise your chance of a win, there are certain situations where sharing will benefit you. I'm talking about prize draws hosted using an app with a viral share option like Woobox, Gleam, Rafflecopter or Offerpop – or competitions where you need votes to win.

Referral prize draws

With a referral promotion, you get a bonus entry in the draw for any friend that enters after clicking on your unique reference link. Usually after entering, you'll be assigned a unique web link and can choose to copy it, share it on various social networks or send via email to a friend.

If, like me, you have a large network of prize-hungry friends this is an excellent way of increasing your entries in a draw. The promoter will be pleased because of the big entry numbers, your mates will be happy as they've discovered a new competition via your post or tweet – and you'll be delighted because you have a few more entries in the virtual hat.

If it's a prize you really want, increase your chances of winning by sharing the referral link on Facebook and Twitter daily. Bookmark the unique link into a daily folder, or use an app like **Tweetdeck** or **Hootsuite** to schedule tweets and Facebook posts to send when you're not around. Stick to sharing this unique link on your own Facebook profile, blog or Twitter feed. If you share your unique referral link in a group or on a forum, don't post it as a *"dirty link"*, without mentioning you will gain from it. Be honest and let people know you get an extra entry if they use your link to enter – check the forum rules before you post though, as some only allow posting a *"clean link"* directly to the app.

You can find referral comps on a Twitter search by looking for *Woobox*, or look out for Facebook notifications from your friends via the *Sweepstakes* app. Sometimes you won't know if it is a referral comp until you've actually entered, and are presented with a unique sharing link.

Voting competitions

It's hard for me to say a good word about voting competitions, having seen the havoc they can wreak (see tip 93, **Don't enter voting competitions**). Obviously, if you've entered a voting competition, it pays to share your entry everywhere you possibly can – but keep in mind it's remarkably hard to get people to vote without there being some form of incentive (eg. every voter has the chance of winning a prize). The only fair voting competition is one where every entrant who has received a set number of votes (10 or 20 is reasonable) is entered either into a random draw for the prize, or is judged on merit.

If you do want to try a voting competition, my advice would be to message or email each friend individually and ask them politely if they wouldn't mind voting. Unless you have friends in the same competition, do this in the last few days of the promotion. It's a waste of your time doing it at the beginning – most entrants who lead at the start of a voting competition won't go on to win it as they will run out of steam by the end. Share your link widely in the last 24 hours – there's a thrilling sense of urgency at the end of a voting competition, and if you can make your friends a part of that excitement they will be more inclined to help you out. Check the T&Cs of a voting competition very carefully – it's usually a fine line between what's acceptable and what isn't, and you should ask the promoter up front if you have any queries.

58. Learn to keep a secret

Yes, I know this is a little confusing – keeping a secret is the opposite to sharing the love! But there's a time and place for sharing competition details, and if you want to win bigger, better prizes, sharing is definitely *not* the way to go.

I believe in comping karma, and what goes around comes around. I love to share details of comps and prize draws, but there *are* situations where I'm desperate to win a certain prize, so I stay quiet.

Instant win or purchase necessary promotions are a great example – if you discover a great new comp with daily prizes, keep entering until you win. *Then* share it with fellow compers. Why spoil your chance of a prize by letting everyone else join the fun early?

Pinterest secret boards

If you're already comping on Pinterest you'll know that prize promotions on the platform are low entry and generally hard to find. So if you *do* manage to find a Pinterest competition that's low entry, you probably don't want everybody else to find out about it – and you definitely don't want other lazy entrants repinning your photos to their own boards.

That's where **secret boards** on Pinterest come in handy. You can set up a maximum of three, and I always use them for my own competition entries. When you create a public board, your friends on Pinterest get a notification – so they'll see your board title and know about the competition straight away. And when you comment with a link to your board on a competition pin, or tweet it with the competition hashtag, all the other entrants can follow your link or click the hashtag and have a good look at your board before they create their own. They might even dare to repin some of the photos on *your* board onto theirs!

So, do as I do. Create your board set to Secret, add all your pins and get everything ready to go – then hold fire until the day before the closing date (or even the closing date, if you dare). Click *Edit board* at the top and change the setting on *Keep it Secret?* from *Yes* to *No*. Hopefully by this time anyone who spots your new board won't have time to rustle up anything near as fabulous. It's a good idea to set a phone or calendar reminder to change your board setting – you wouldn't want to put the effort in only to forget all about entering.

Don't share on Facebook

One of the things that puzzles me most about Facebook is the people who share every competition they enter. When you share, it pushes the post to the tickers and news feeds of your friends, as well as to your profile page. That's brilliant for a referral comp – but in most cases, you're reducing your chances in the comp as dozens of your mates click through to enter. That's why Like & Share promotions are so difficult to win – they get too many entries!

When you post on your own timeline, you can choose who to share with from the drop-down menu at the bottom of the box you type in – the privacy setting will usually be set to *Public* or *Friends.*

If you're entering a prize draw via a Facebook app or Facebook login on a website, you can sometimes share for an extra entry. Did you know you can set this share to **Only Me**? The app will register it as a share and will give you a bonus entry in the draw, but you're the only person that will see it. Be aware that Facebook remembers your sharing setting, and will use it for your next post – but you can go back and change the privacy setting of a post at any time.

If it's a Like & Share prize draw, you *should* share on the **Public** setting – a share restricted to a list won't be seen by the promoter (see my video demonstrating this at **www.superlucky. me/SharingDemo**). From experience though, I know that many promoters won't even look at the shares list – they choose a winner from the likes or comments instead, because it's easier. I've tested this theory myself, and won two 'Like & Share' draws with my share set to the *'Only Me'* setting. My tip would be to share on the *'Only Me'* setting – and then if you're lucky enough to win, find the competition photo on your profile page and change the privacy from *'Only Me'* to *'Public'* – in case anyone queries it. This also means you won't infuriate your non-comping Facebook friends with lots of sharing.

On Facebook, Twitter and Instagram when you encounter a low entry comp you really want to win, bookmark it and set a reminder in your calendar to post your entry at the very last minute. This means anyone who sees your comment, photo or like on their news feed or Facebook ticker will be too late to join the party!

Finally, if you win a comp you've kept to yourself, don't feel guilty. To quote the successful comper Bobby Green (sadly no longer with us), a low entry promotion is *"the holy grail of competitions"* and if you find one occasionally and win it, you should feel proud. Sometimes I might decide to keep a low entry comp to myself (which is getting harder, believe me!) but if I do win I always promise the promoter I'll help spread the word about their next giveaway.

59. Choose your entry time carefully

Some compers always leave everything to the last minute, panicking on the final day of the month when the PrizeFinder website has 500 competitions in the *Closing Today* category! Others prefer to enter new comps as soon as they spot them. I like to do a little of both – it really does depend on the type of promotion you're entering.

Postal competitions

Back when the UK postal service was more reliable, I always posted my newspaper and magazine entries with a first class stamp the day before the closing date. My theory was that all the other entries would be sitting in a box somewhere, then my brightly-coloured, homemade entry would arrive on the desk as a reminder that the winner needed to be drawn – and the person doing it would be too lazy to choose any entry but mine. I won a lot of prize draws with this method – I've even risked posting entries *on* the closing date, and still won a couple of times, so it's never too late to try!

"In 1996 I found a good slogan competition to win a car in SHE magazine. It had already closed, but I had a good slogan in mind and sent it off anyway. That was how I won my second car, a Daewoo Nexia!" – Janet Leng

---

I don't leave my postal entries to the last minute any more – but I do still try and send off postal entries to arrive on a Friday. Why? I like to think the person selecting the winner will be in a much better mood on a Friday – and maybe that's why so many winning telephone calls are made on a Friday too.

Online prize draws and competitions

If you use a competition listings site, try not to put yourself under the pressure of entering the 'closing today' comps. On the 31st of the month you'll end up stressed out, wasting time clicking links to comps that have already closed. It's better to look at what's *new* on the site each day. For 'referral' prize draws, you should enter and share as soon as you can – the same goes for prize draws with a daily entry or daily tweet option.

Creative competitions

You may be tempted to leave your entry to the very last minute for a photo competition, in case someone steals your amazing idea – but don't leave it too late if it's on an app or blog! Your entry may need to be moderated by the promoter to ensure it's suitable for publication – if you enter at the very last minute you're taking a risk. Sometimes it can take more than 24 hours for a video or a blog comment to be moderated and published: set a reminder in your calendar or diary to check the following day that your entry is there.

On-pack promotions and instant wins

If you spot a new on-pack code promotion which is an instant win, or daily prize draw, buy it and enter the code as soon as you can (to find out if it's new, search competition forums to see if it's listed yet). Some promotional packaging only makes it to supermarket shelves after the promotion has started. If prizes are awarded after winning moments, and after a week there have been no codes entered, there will be a backlog of prizes and every code entered for a certain amount of time should (in theory) be a winner. It's the same for daily draws – if the packs are slow to reach the shops, yet you've found them in your local supermarket, stock up and get your entries in early!

Most on-pack promotions are advertised way before the promotion launches, giving the packs time to get to the shops and making sure people know when the daily draws or the instant wins start. In this case, lots of people will be entering enthusiastically on those first few days. If you can resist the temptation, buy the promotional packs and hold on to your codes until the very end of the promotion – by this time, the people who spent all that money at the start will be tiring of it, plus the promotional coded packs might well have disappeared from the shelves.

When you should enter immediately

If it's a referral prize draw, you should enter the minute you see it – every friend that clicks your unique share link to enter the prize draw will gain you another entry, so you should send the link out multiple times before your other friends hear about it. There are also a few comps where the first people to comment, tweet or upload a photo will win prizes.

When you should enter at the last minute

Entering competitions at the last minute is the best strategy for Facebook, Twitter Instagram and Pinterest, where entries are public. This is for two reasons. Firstly, a late entry reduces the chance of your followers seeing your entry and having time to enter too. Secondly, the promoter may not be choosing winners fairly and only checking the list of the most recent comments, shares, retweets or replies.

It's difficult and costly to choose a random Twitter RT winner from a database of every single entry, so many promoters will choose manually. Entering a Twitter prize draw in the last ten minutes can pay off as your entry will be at the top of the promoter's replies or retweets list, and is more likely to be chosen than older entries from the start of the competition. The same applies to Facebook timeline promotions.

60. Interact with brands

Getting on friendly terms with promoters and brands is beneficial when it comes to winning competitions. Position yourself as a dedicated fan of a brand – without doing anything too cringeworthy – and you should eventually benefit. If there's a competition you really have your heart set on, make sure you've researched the brand thoroughly. Turn on notifications for their tweets (set this via the settings/gear icon on a profile page), and their Facebook posts (click *Liked*, then *Get notifications*). Interacting can be as simple as replying to chatty tweets, commenting on Instagram photos, a Facebook like or comment. There should be at least one or two companies that you feel passionately about and it's nice to let them know you care.

Commenting is a good way to gain an advantage in a Facebook timeline promotion, particularly if your words are relevant or witty. Don't make it too obvious that you're a comper – you want the company to see you're a fan of their brand (yes – even if you've never heard of *Passionate popcorn* before in your life!)

Local companies will regularly pick familiar names as winners in their Facebook comps – much to the dismay of other entrants. But if you love your local pub, restaurant or beauty salon, take advantage of this – your genuine appreciation should stand out above a sea of 'Liked & Shared' comments.

If you listen to the radio, get in touch for song requests or fun text-ins as well as competitions – your name is sometimes stored with your number on the system. If they're choosing an entrant to call back, seeing a regular listener on the spreadsheet might sway them. I remember winning some vinyl on Kerrang! Radio a few years ago – when the DJ answered with *"Hello there Di – previous £1,000 winner!*", I was shocked. I'd won £1,000 five years beforehand, and that was what they'd saved with my number on their system!

61. Have a sense of humour

You'll definitely be more successful if you approach your hobby with an open mind and a sense of humour. I've won some amazing prizes by making a fool of myself – creative comping adds an element of surprise to your life. If you can relax and have a laugh then you'll also be a great candidate for radio comps or TV game shows, where the big money is.

Finding a creative comping partner can be incredibly useful – if you have a friend who's up for a giggle then try and get them on board. I've converted several of my fun-loving friends into compers, and am proud to say that their creative efforts are often outstanding.

You may feel embarrassed sharing selfies on Facebook or Twitter at first, but remember that making people smile can never be a bad thing. Embarrassing comps get very low entry numbers (for a good reason!) but that means you have a brilliant chance of winning. This year Vimto asked for selfies where you stuck out your tongue like the #Vimtoad, and several SuperLucky fans were lucky iPad winners in this low entry daily draw. I'll never forget dressing as a banana for a TopFruit video competition and stripping to a Wonderwoman outfit in a car showroom (you can watch these at **www.youtube.com/superluckydi**) – I didn't win either of these incredibly low-entry comps but my neighbours, family and friends certainly enjoyed the experiences!

On the subject of dressing up, collect as many fancy dress items and accessories as you can. Novelty sunglasses, wigs and hats can transform a simple selfie into something colourful and special. Props can be lots of fun too – I have a box full of fake moustaches, 80s party frocks, pirate outfits, Snazaroo face paint and a genie's magic lamp. I'm still waiting for the right competition to dust off my lamp!

"I don't know whether it's advice given or just Di leading by example... if you're going to spend time entering competitions you may as well have fun! I've had (numerous) buckets of water thrown over me, been slapped in the face by a fish, played discus with a Rod Stewart album in a supermarket car park and American Football in another... I've spent far too much time frantically driving around to find a spot for 'the perfect photo' and I have a box of comping things which includes blow-up dolls. It makes it easier that I tend to enter with my good friend Lisa. We try wherever possible to both enter with different ideas and then share our prize. It's led us to doing some fantastic things from amazing hospitality at the Olympics, to holidays and thousands of pounds in cash!"– Laura M

62. Enter kids' competitions

My very first competition win was a VIP weekend in London when I was six, a prize from a colouring competition sponsored by the local newspaper. It was to celebrate the Queen Mother's 80th birthday and I spent long hours scribbling away with my felt tips. You can read the story and see my unusual artwork at **www. superlucky.me/MyFirstWin**.

I didn't pay too much attention to kids' competitions until I had a child of my own and discovered the appeal of the comics section of WHSmith. Kids' magazines will set you back a few quid so do your research before buying – make sure you're getting entertainment for the child PLUS an opportunity to win a prize. With a bit of research I learnt which magazines and comics are the best bet for winning prizes – look out for:

- Entry forms that must be posted off.

- Drawing and colouring competitions, particularly where you have to draw on a page from the comic.

- Letters pages with lots of prizes.

- Postcard entry competitions.

- Brand new titles.

Comics and magazines that offer an email entry option will find their way onto competition forums and websites, and get lots more entries. You should still enter them of course, but don't expect to win as easily!

I usually have a flick through several comics (the ones that aren't frustratingly encased in plastic) to choose a couple of good ones. If I spot a postal or email entry comp but feel it's not worth buying the comic, I discreetly take a photo with my phone (see tip 11, **Make the most of your smartphone**).

Take the entry forms and drawing competitions out of the comic as soon as you can, or they will get lost under all the toys in the kids' room. I usually sit with Ryland straight away to work out any answers or puzzles. If you're posting off an entry, get your kids to draw or put stickers on the postcard or envelope. If they're old enough, get them to write out their own name and address details, plus the address on the envelope – if they're too young for that, perhaps you could get them to just write their name. The recipient might favour an entry where the child has clearly done it themselves.

There are also a great number of websites focusing on competitions for kids – go for the ones where you need to put in a date of birth, and try and encourage the kids to enter themselves – it's never too soon to get them interested in the hobby. Sign them up to join the free Lego club; their regular magazine has exclusive fun photo comps for members.

Look out for creative children's competitions – there are photo, video, blogging and cooking competitions that require the kids to do fun things, and these type of effort comps are brilliant if you have time to fill in the holidays. Writing competitions are a fabulous way to keep them practising over the long summer break – get them to keep a holiday diary as you may be able to use the photos and stories in comps. If you have babies or toddlers, that shouldn't stop you from entering art competitions – Ry won several prizes with messy glittery collages when he was very young. If your child creates a Lego masterpiece, decorates a cupcake or draws a beautiful castle, always take a photo as there's sure to be a competition you can enter it in – take a photo of the project alone, then a second photo including your child.

We've spent hours making loo roll heroes, marble runs, recycled cars, hats, Lego creations, fun biscuits and more – and have won some fantastic prizes as a result, even bagging a £3,500 holiday with Ryland's pasta recipe (in a video comp with less than 15 entries). If creative kids' competitions are your thing, check **www. superlucky.me** for my regular round-ups of UK comps for the school holidays.

"Last weekend we had afternoon tea with Mary Berry because my eight-year-old son won the junior bakes category of the Bakes and Cakes show. I would never in a million years have imagined that I'd meet Mary Berry – but he just entered his bake on the off-chance and he won!" – Rebecca B

---

63. Love your selfie

If you're shy, look away now! When it comes to photo competitions, selfies are still incredibly popular – and as most entries need to be shared in public on social media, camera-shy compers need not apply.

All over the world, promoters are asking people to upload selfies featuring their product in order to win a prize – or perhaps they might want to see a selfie taken in their shop or restaurant. There are pub selfies, pet selfies and even feet selfies to keep you busy – some companies have even invented their own twist on the selfie, such as a #yawnie or #shoefie. The great thing about selfies is that the entrant *must* feature in the photo – making it hard for cheeky cheats to Google for a photo to use.

But what exactly *is* a selfie? Most people consider a selfie to be a photo taken on a phone with a front-facing camera, using an outstretched arm – or of course, a selfie stick. Most promoters aren't strict about the method used, and the terms and conditions will rarely specify exactly what kind of selfie it should be. If you prefer, you could submit a more formal self-portrait, taken using a tripod with self-timer or remote control.

To take a selfie on a phone or tablet, tap the on-screen icon (usually two arrows in a camera) to change the direction of your camera from back-facing to front-facing. The resolution of the photo is lower using the front-facing camera, but you'll find it much easier to get the right composition if you can see yourself on the screen.

If you don't have a camera on your phone, you can take a selfie with a digital camera, a tablet or a computer webcam.

I had a lovely win of an iPhone with a selfie featuring a box of Silver Bay Point Wine. There were less than 50 entries submitted (some of these were from the same family!) and ten iPhones to be won – that's fantastic odds for the price of a wine box.

Selfie tips

- There are usually a couple of ways you can take your photo – you might find it easier to press a button on the side (on an iPhone it's the volume button) rather than tap the screen to take the photo.

- Experiment with different angles to find which is your good side – swap hands to see which looks best.

- Set your camera to square format so it will be Instagram-ready without having to crop out important bits.

- Taking a photo from slightly above eye level is the most flattering.

- If you get really stuck squeezing in all the elements you need to (jeans, random product, celebrity, etc.) then ask someone to help, but make sure they're close enough to you so the photo still looks like a 'proper' selfie.

- If there's more than one person in the shot, it looks better with eyes at the same level and heads together.

- Take your selfie in natural light. Don't use the flash, it will make you look twenty years older!

- Check the background isn't too distracting.

- If the selfie must feature a specific product or location, make sure it's in shot.

- On an iPhone, tap the circles icon at the bottom right of your camera app to see instant filters which you can apply before you take your shot, including black & white and sepia effects.

- In Instagram or Twitter you can add filters to your photo before sharing it – test them out to see which work best. Some of them can even magically make you look younger.

- Use a selfie stick. These remote-controlled gadgets have been banned from many tourist attractions and football grounds, but as long as you take care then it might be just what you need for the perfect prize-winning photo.

- Use a remote control for your camera – these are handy and cheap.

- Use a self-timer and prop your phone up somewhere safe (or use a tripod). Tap the clock icon on your iPhone camera app, or use a free app like **Timercam** or **Gorillacam**. Tap the button and you have a few seconds to get into position, so you don't need to worry about holding the phone still *and* pressing the button.

- Sometimes your selfie might get photo-bombed. Don't dismiss a photo just because it has someone else lurking in the back – if it's funny that could help you win!

- Being serious in a selfie only really works if you're a celebrity – and even then, it can often be more hilarious than sultry. Smile and have a bit of fun – a wink or a fun facial expression shows your character.

64. Recycle your creative ideas

Don't feel too disappointed if your incredible slogan or photo doesn't win a prize – after all, sometimes the judges can have an off day! Entries can usually be recycled. Read the rules carefully first: some will state that you can't enter with a photo that has previously been entered in a competition. This won't be a problem if you remembered to take lots of alternative photos when you did your shoot.

Use a notebook – or even better, the *Notes* function on your smartphone (or the brilliant **Evernote** app) to store competition entries safely. There are lots of topics that appear year after year – poems and stories for Valentine's Day, Mother's Day and Father's Day, stories about your best friend, DIY disasters, top tips about beauty, travel and money saving, and your best holiday story are all regular themes on Facebook and Twitter, and you can re-use old ideas with a few tweaks here and there.

If the promoter gives you a choice of entry methods for photo or video comps, consider uploading to Instagram or Vine with a short caption that doesn't reference the comp. Then to enter, send a link to the photo/video via Twitter and add the competition hashtag to your tweet. You'll still have that video/photo to use for other comps without it being obvious it was created for a specific promotion (eg. for your pumpkin photos at Halloween). On Instagram you can also add new hashtags to old photos – but keep in mind the promoter may be checking the entry was uploaded since the competition started. It's better to upload the photo again with a slightly different crop or filter.

A great way to recycle losing entries is to send them in to magazines – in the UK email your recipe photos to mags like Delicious or My Favourite Recipes, and send your silly photos to women's weeklies to win cash prizes.

It's hard to justify spending money on a prop or costume just to enter a creative competition, but in many cases you can recycle those too. Years ago I splashed out on two fun Abba wigs and sang 'Mamma Mia' for a Maoam video competition, but was frustrated when my entry wasn't even shown in the gallery! Since then I've worn the wigs for lots of other photo and video comps and have won several prizes, including £200 cash from eBay and a £100 Amazon gift card.

"On holiday with my best friend in Disney World, we realised that she pulled the most iconic expressions on the rides. I took a selfie as we whizzed around Big Thunder Mountain Railroad – it wasn't till we looked back at the photo later that we cracked up laughing. We sent it to The Sun for their 'best holiday photo' competition, and won £150 of hotels.com vouchers. Not long after that, Taste inc asked for the funniest photo you could find to win an Xbox One, I couldn't believe it when it won again! Since then, the photo has won me £300 of Lowcostholidays vouchers, an Alton Towers break, £450 lastminute vouchers, a Teapigs and Thomas J Fudge bundle and a selfie stick!" – Elysia Benn

65. Know the comping calendar

Each year promoters stick to the same predictable themes for their competitions, but that's great because it means *you* can be prepared. On Pancake Day and Halloween, you'll see hundreds of promoters asking for photos of our amazing creations, when realistically most people are too busy cooking or carving to consider taking a photo of their masterpiece. A comper, on the other hand, will spend time in the weeks before the event making sure their entry is perfect – or they can always use photos they took the previous year.

If you enjoy occasions and celebrations then you'll be a natural with themed competitions. Go all out at Halloween and Christmas with face paints, lights, baking and fancy dress. Buy cheap decorations and gimmicks after the event to put aside for the following year. Use Pinterest to find inspiration for fancy dress, unusual make-up and creative food, and pin the best photos to themed boards.

Here are a few of the UK's top occasions for themed competitions:

New Year

What's your New Year's Resolution? Think of something unique and interesting – promoters always want to know what it is, and most people leave predictable answers like 'do more exercise' and 'eat healthily'. For 2015 mine was to get a book published – I managed two!

Blue Monday

#BlueMonday is the third Monday of the year, so called because it's the most miserable day of the year when the Christmas bills come in. This year, the BlueMonday hashtag had lots of photo and tiebreaker comps.

Valentine's Day

On Valentine's Day you'll be asked to share photos of your loved one, first date (and worst date) stories, poems, romantic meals and random heart-shaped things.

Mother's Day

For Mother's Day, prepare a selfie of you and your mum, and scan in old photos of your mum with you as a baby. You might be asked to write poems and share touching memories.

Pancake Day

Conjure up unusual pancake fillings and recipes, and make your pancakes into works of art using food dye and decorations. Videos of pancake flipping are in demand – keep them short as you'll probably have to share on Vine (6 seconds max) or Instagram (15 seconds max). Tossing the pancake out of shot or sticking it to the ceiling is always fun!

Red Nose Day

Red Nose Day is held every other March in the UK, and a good excuse for funny face and joke competitions as well as charity raffles with big prizes.

Easter

Online virtual egg hunts are popular. Don't have time to find the eggs? Check competition forums to see if somebody else has already done it for you! There's also egg painting, Easter bonnets and a ton of estimation competitions. I'm actually considering buying a glass jar and filling it with chocolate eggs so I can estimate more accurately next year!

Summer

Look out for competitions with a barbecue, picnic, summer or seaside theme – build creative sandcastles on the beach and take lots of nature photos. On the beach, get a photo of you and the family splashing in the sea or jumping in the air. Writing words in the sand – especially product names – works a treat as it's clear you've taken a photo for that specific competition.

Wimbledon

Everyone in the UK goes crazy for Wimbledon – and there are lots of tennis-themed photo comps to enter. Champagne and strawberries might be worth including!

World Cup (football, rugby, cricket)

Show your support for your national team – usually in the form of a photo, video or song. Face painting always looks great! Check Twitter during the matches too – guessing scores is a popular theme for competitions.

Back to school

Be sure to take a photo of your little one looking smart on the first day of school term, and search for photo comps with the #BackToSchool hashtag.

Halloween

Halloween competitions usually involve pumpkin carving and decoration, or fancy dress. To make your entry stand out from the crowd, take inspiration from someone (or something!) funny or topical. You can find lots of excellent zombie make-up and fancy dress ideas on YouTube and Pinterest – my baby mummy costume for Ryland won us over £1,000 of prizes!

Movember

Movember is a campaign to get men to grow a moustache during the month of November, raising funds for vital men's health programmes. Movember goes from strength to strength each year – which is why so many companies love running competitions to promote it. Even if you can't grow your own moustache, there are Movember prizes for ladies, pets and more – just use your imagination, stick a bit of fuzz on your lip or get your felt tips out. I won several prizes with my eyeliner moustache, including a trip to Amsterdam.

Christmas/Advent

On December 1st, prepare for the most exhausting time of a comper's year. See the next section for advice on how to survive the onslaught of daily prizes. When you tire of the dailies, look out for Christmas jumper and Christmas tree photo competitions – I win at least a couple of these every year with a new photo of my hideous 1980s appliquéed jumper.

"I won a total of eight lovely prizes for my Mum this year from the Mother's Day comps posted on SuperLucky. Most of them were effort comps which I wrote a poem for. My prizes included a luxury spa break, afternoon tea hamper, magnum of champagne (aptly named 'Mumm'), a box of Clarins products and a meal for four with champagne and flowers. Mum was over the moon especially as I don't see her very often and wasn't able to visit her on Mother's Day" – Liz

---

66. Prepare for Advent

There will be *hundreds* of daily December comps on websites, Facebook and Twitter. Some of them will offer a prize every day, and some of them will only be running on weekdays – usually from 1st to 24th December. There are also '12 days of Christmas' promotions, although these usually start on the 1st or 12th December, rather than the correct date of the 25th. Scrolling through a full list of Advent comps daily is time-consuming, when you probably only want to enter a small percentage, so use browser bookmarks to organise them.

Bookmarking

- Create a new bookmark folder called *Advents*. Inside this, you could create more folders, eg. *Essential Advents* for the ones you definitely want to enter daily. You could create *Web*, *FB* and *Twitter* folders – and *'Essential web'*, *'Essential FB'* and *'Essential Twitter'*. If you're short on time, simply do the essentials.

- To find comps to bookmark, start with the Advent category at **www.theprizefinder.com**, which will be live from 1st December. Go through the list visiting each website, and decide if that's a comp you'll be interested in doing daily. If so, add it to your essential folder. Do the same with the competitions posted on forums and in Facebook groups – plus any others you spot on the internet or social media.

- Do the comps in your Advents folder daily – right-click the folder and use the **Open all Bookmarks** shortcut to open all links in new tabs, then close as you work through them. Try to restrict the number of bookmarks in each folder so you don't have too many tabs opening at once – split the links across several folders if you need to.

- Check for new additions to the Advent comps each day on comping sites and if appropriate, add to your bookmarks.

- Delete bookmarks for closed comps.

Tips

- If you choose the same time daily to do your Advents, it's best to do them after 10am and before 5pm – some promoters only launch at 10am, and some close their giveaways at 5pm!

- If you're going to enter hundreds of Advents, consider breaking your folders down into times too, eg. *'enter after 10am'*, *'enter before 5pm'*.

- Using your browser's **Autofill** function or downloading **RoboForm** will save you time.

- Some promoters don't give you much time to claim the prize, so check for wins regularly (see the **Finding your wins** section for advice).

Finally, don't get stressed out by Advents – *nobody* has enough time to enter them all. Lots of people take up comping in December because the lure of the daily prizes is so strong – but you will be better off bookmarking a handful of daily prize draws to enter, and focus your time on the festive creative competitions instead. I don't enter many Advent comps myself but I get at least three wins each year – last year I won a smart dinner service from Kaleidoscope.

67. Use your talents

Comping is a wonderfully varied hobby where you can use your skills or your job to win you prizes in all sorts of situations. Here are just a few ideas.

- **Good at pub quizzes or general knowledge?** Apply for a **TV gameshow,** or try the *'ten questions to win £1,000'* type quizzes on the **radio.**

- **Are you an incredible cook?** Look out for recipe competitions – and be sure to photograph *everything* you make. Instagram should be your social network of choice!

- **Builder or plumber?** Check trade publications and look for in-store promotions – vans and power tools are popular prizes. When our friendly plumber cleaned our central heating with a promotional bottle of Fernox, little did we know we would end up travelling to the Brazilian Grand Prix after winning the slogan competition advertised on the bottle!

- **Bartender?** Look out for cocktail competitions and promotions in local bars and nightclubs – you could soon find yourself rustling up mojitos in America!

- **Newsagent?** Check the newspapers and magazines for comps – you can find some great low-entry comps tucked away in local papers and even the national dailies.

- **Sporty type?** Look out for competitions where you enter as a team – it's hard to organise people to do this, so the odds of winning are good.

- **Designer or film-maker?** Look for design comps – **www. eyeka.com** has some great cash prizes available to global entrants.

- **Fashionista?** Learn to use moodboard apps like Polyvore or ASAP54 and take lots of blogger-style photos of your #OOTD (Outfit Of The Day). Fashion bloggers have an advantage in photo competitions because they always look so impeccably styled – yet many of them don't bother to enter comps.

- **Hairdresser, nail artist or beautician?** Take photos of your best creations (ask your model/client for permission first).

An office job can be useful, and you might want to check for promotional items in the stationery cupboard, or competitions in the catalogues that arrive. When I worked as a designer, I used to do the monthly office stationery order. Acco were offering prizes for ordering certain products, so I checked with my boss if it was okay for me to buy a specific brand of staples for a qualifying receipt. Each month there was a tiebreaker competition and I entered three months in a row, spending a whopping £4.50 on staples in total. One Friday I took a call at the office to say I'd won the quarterly prize of £2,000 cash. I was gobsmacked – and had to ask my understanding boss for time off to collect my giant prize cheque!

68. Be a man about it

There are far fewer men entering comps than women, and for products like Gillette Razors and Lynx, football magazines and TalkSport, the promoter is targeting men and will prefer a male winner. For some comps – particularly postal ones – you could always just use your initial so the promoter doesn't know what sex you are.

If you're female, you should ask the men in your life if it's okay to put their details down for a comp – but warn them about a possible winning phone call or email. Luckily Rob is fully trained in the etiquette, having taken winning phone calls for a holiday to Brazil, football kit for his team and a day's cooking with Heston Blumenthal. Actually, he did write the tiebreaker and postcard for the Heston competition himself – with me standing over him, making sure he did it. Generally though, I'll be grabbing his phone and texting the entries myself when he's not looking!

Sending off postcards and completing email entries is easy to do on someone else's behalf, but a husband, son or brother might not appreciate you doing the same on his social media accounts. Ask nicely and he might agree to sending the odd Twitter, Facebook or Instagram competition entry, if there's a good chance of a win and he can delete it later on – or he may be happy for you to set up a new Twitter account on his behalf just for competition entries. Wilkinson offered a hundred prize vouchers in a recent competition where you had to take a selfie in the men's department, and they couldn't give away all the prizes because entry numbers were so low. It's just a fact that most men aren't as comp-crazy as women, and that can give fellas a big advantage if they do take up the hobby seriously.

If you're a man who likes comping then make the most of it – start chatting, commenting and liking on social media as much as you can. Men's magazines, shops, websites and brands are desperate for decent interaction from their target audience – search for your favourite drinks and snacks on Facebook and Twitter, and you'll see many of them running comps. Men might also get lucky with competitions aimed at ladies, if they submit a funny or cheeky entry!

"I get to know my postman on a first name basis, every day could potentially be Christmas, every Twitter notification, Facebook notification or email is potentially worth thousands, and to all intents and purposes it's a zero investment hobby. There IS such thing as a free lunch, I've been there and had the slap-up meal a few times now." –
Michael Scoates

---

69. Get on a game show

If you've taken the plunge and found a TV gameshow you want to apply for (see tip 33), here are a few tips on making an impression at the audition and getting a step closer to winning your fortune.

- **Find a partner.** Lots of shows need pairs – Million Pound Drop, Pointless and many of the BBC Lottery shows. If possible, pair up with someone who has different strengths to you, to cover all topics.

- **Take time on your application and photo.** Often the production company will want to know fun facts and stories about you – this is what makes your application stand out, so try and write something memorable. Don't attach a passport photo, but find one where you're smiling naturally.

- **Relax.** Be prepared to get a phone call almost as soon as you've sent off your application. When they call, be enthusiastic and chatty. You'll be asked why you want to appear on the show, so make sure you've done your research. They will usually ask you a few general knowledge questions. *You don't need to get* *these right* – in most cases, it's better if you *don't* get them all right. At the end of the phone call if you've impressed them they will invite you to audition – it will usually be a hotel in your nearest large city and last a couple of hours. Make yourself look presentable, and if possible wear something to make you memorable. Think carefully in advance about what to say – you need to stand out, but you also need the viewers to be able to relate to you. Get there early and chat to fellow contestants – it will help you relax and you might even get tips from some of the pros who've been on lots of shows. Usually you will do a run-through of the show, a written quiz and be interviewed privately on camera. If it's a multiple choice question, it's important to talk through the elimination of incorrect answers before giving your answer.

- **Enjoy your 15 minutes of fame!** If you get onto the show, try and relax. You'll spend a lot of time in the 'Green Room' with the other contestants – chat as much as possible so you're comfortable with them and can have a laugh during the breaks in filming. Remember it's a once-in-a-lifetime experience that you can tell stories about for years to come, so savour every moment. If you fluff an answer it's embarrassing, but it makes you human. If you're talking to the presenter, use their name. Tell short, funny stories and don't waffle nervously – try and be natural, as if you're amongst friends. It gets easier with every show – honestly!

- **Think positive.** My first experience of a game show was *The Price is Right*. Every audience member did a short interview on the way into the studio. I *knew* I would be one of the few picked to 'come on down' – and I was. I didn't win anything mind you, but since my TV debut I've won over £10,000 on game shows – I like to think of *The Price is Right* as my practice run!

Finally, if you don't do well on the show – try not to have regrets. It's good practice – and eventually you *will* win! For more tips on

135

game shows read my blog post of top tips at **www.superlucky. me/2014/03/top-tips-get-on-a-tv-game-show/**.

70. Start a blog

This isn't a quick, easy tip to put into practice but if you're dedicated, it can result in a lot of prizes and enjoyment. There are lots of promotions with big prizes that are only open to bloggers – some are random prize draws, so there's no need to worry about writing an award-winning post. Usually you need to write a post on a specific topic and include a link to the competition details – then complete your entry by adding the link to a 'linky' list, or tweeting it with a unique hashtag.

In a judged competition, compers' blogs are often overlooked – if it's a fashion, travel or beauty themed challenge then it's likely a more specialised blogger will win. Competitions with a general lifestyle or family theme are more appropriate – I've had success with blog posts about iPhone apps, my favourite music and baking with kids! If winners are picked at random though, it shouldn't make any difference what your blog is about – so go for it.

You can find current blogging comps listed on **www.britmums. com** or **www.tots100.co.uk**. Sometimes you'll have to be a member of the site (blogging competitions are mainly aimed at parent bloggers). Other UK companies who run blogging comps regularly are *Debenhams*, *Heart Home magazine* and *Hillarys* – or search Google or Twitter for *'blogger competition'*.

Tips on starting your first blog

- **Decide why you're blogging.** It's not a great idea to blog simply so you can enter blogging competitions. Blogging is actually a great hobby! Do your research and check out other blogs before deciding on a theme for your own.

- **Avoid referencing comping** – some of the promoters or agencies won't be keen on awarding a prize to a comping blogger.

- **Come up with a good name** – ideally a fairly short one. You might want to come up with a blog name based on your Twitter or Instagram name.

- **Decide whether to use Blogger or Wordpress.** For beginners, Blogger (owned by Google) is much easier to get to grips with. A free Wordpress blog has a lot of restrictions – you can't monetise the blog, or embed giveaway widgets like Rafflecopter or Gleam. I started with Blogger but when SuperLucky became more than just a hobby blog, I needed the options that a self-hosted (paid for) Wordpress blog offered me.

- **Choose a theme** – you can find free themes online or pay a minimal amount for a smart one – make sure it's mobile-friendly.

- **Write your About page** – this is where promoters and PR agencies will head to first, so make sure it's positive and well written, with a nice photo.

- **Set up categories** and start writing posts for each of these categories so there's something for people to read when they arrive at your site.

- **Promote yourself on social media** – and by commenting on other blogs, where possible leaving a link back to yours.

- **Host giveaways** – running giveaways will increase your traffic, social media followers and help you establish relationships with brands and PRs. If this is something you're interested in, read my e-book *'Blog Giveaways – The ultimate guide to hosting prize draws and competitions on your blog'* which you can purchase for just £1.99 at **www.superlucky.me/BGbook**.

- **Post as often as you feel like it** – once a week is enough.

"I won the top prize of £250 cash in the Taylor Wimpey Dinner Party menu competition. I actually couldn't believe it and nearly fell off my chair when they called! This was the first blogger competition I won and inspired me to keep going and enter more. Lots of the entries were quirky, but I decided to blog about my favourite food items and it paid off. From this, I learnt to always be yourself with your entries!" – Hannah Igoe

Tools of the trade

There are certain applications and software which will make your comping life easier – and in most cases they won't cost you a penny. This section introduces my own personal favourites.

71. Race through entries with RoboForm

RoboForm is an application which makes password management and form-filling fast and simple across all your devices – allowing you to log in to websites quickly and easily on your phone, tablet or computer. It's a huge time-saver for compers.

RoboForm is much more powerful than your browser's Autofill function, with custom fields and the ability to save details for specific entry forms. RoboForm can generate strong, random passwords for you – ideal for websites where you have to use a password with *'more than 8 characters including a number and a capital letter'*.

RoboForm saves **logins** for individual websites – these are your login and password details, allowing you to quickly log in to your favourite forums and websites. RoboForm is powerful for compers as it can save forms for specific websites – for example, if you enter the same prize draw daily, you can tell RoboForm to save the exact form information – then when you visit the site the next day, you can simply load up that information to fill the form with a single click.

RoboForm stores multiple **identities**, so you can add family member details too. On a computer these logins will appear on a toolbar in your browser (except Chrome, which gives you an icon and drop down menu) – simply click the relevant name to fill out a form.

RoboForm custom fields are great for compers – you can specify which text or question RoboForm should look for on a web page, and the text it should fill in (or box it should tick) if it finds it. For example, I have set a custom field *Instagram* which completes with my username *superluckydi*. For tips on using custom fields, see **http://superlucky.me/RoboFormTips**.

RoboForm can be downloaded via my affiliate link at **http://superlucky.me/DownloadRoboform** and is completely free for the first ten website logins/passwords you save. Once you have more than ten, you should upgrade to either *RoboForm Desktop* or *RoboForm Everywhere*. If you only use it for competitions or sweepstakes, the free form-filling function might be all you require – but upgrading does give you unlimited logins and custom fields, which are handy for comping.

If you use a mobile device, download the **RoboForm mobile app** for free at **http://superlucky.me/DownloadRoboformApp**. To access it, use an optional four-digit pin code, and your main RoboForm password – you can change the level of security in your settings if you don't want to input the code and password every time you open the app. Rather than opening a browser on your phone, you browse the internet via the RoboForm app. Tap the home button to see a list of your logins and quickly go to websites, and tap the profile icon to fill forms. Free RoboForm limits you to ten logins.

RoboForm Desktop is a licence for a single computer and requires a one-off payment (currently £19.95), giving you access to unlimited logins and custom fields.

If you comp from multiple devices, it's worth purchasing **RoboForm Everywhere**, which syncs your information in the cloud – this is what I've been using for years. You will need to pay a subscription fee annually (currently £7.95 for the first year, renewing at £13.95) to continue to access your logins across unlimited devices, but with website security measures getting more complex, I believe it's well worth it.

If you're interested in buying RoboForm Desktop or Everywhere, you can download them via my affiliate link at **http://superlucky. me/GetRoboform**.

One of the common queries about RoboForm is whether it's classed as an *automated entry*. Automated entries are actually something entirely different – they are 'third party' entries generated on a large scale. For example, a computer programmed to input 10,000 entries into the same prize draw on behalf of consumers who have paid to subscribe to the service. Many promoters disqualify entries from Automated Entry Services, which is why you'll often see *"Automated entries, bulk entries or third party entries will be disqualified"* in the terms and conditions. If a promoter dislikes automatic form-filling, they can set up their entry form so it won't actually let you use RoboForm or Autofill. In most cases though, promoters really don't mind – it means less chance of an error in the winner's phone number or email address!

Some people get confused when they first start using RoboForm, and you may find the tutorials at **www.roboform.com/tutorials** helpful.

72. Create comping notes using Evernote

Evernote is my favourite app, and I use it to organise every aspect of my life, including comping. It stores individual *notes* in *notebooks* which I can search quickly and easily, and access from any device. Whether it's shopping lists, travel information, school newsletters, loyalty card numbers or photos of promotional codes, Evernote keeps all my essential bits and bobs safely in the cloud.

To get started, sign in with an email and password at **www. evernote.com**. As well as using Evernote via the web, you can download the free app to your computer or mobile device. There's a paid-for Premium version of Evernote, which gives you offline access to notes, but the free version is good enough for compers to get started.

Get started

Click to create a new note, assign it to a notebook and add tags to categorise it. To inspire you, here are a few of the notes I have set up in my *Competitions* notebook:

- **List of creative competitions to do** – Using clickable links, I list 'effort' comps in order by closing date.

- **List of creative competitions entered** – Once I've entered, I move the competition link to this list and will regularly check to see a winner has been announced (if not, I'll chase the promoter!)

- **Purchase-necessary shopping list** – I add products to this list in closing date order, highlighting if they need to be bought at a certain store. I make the product name a clickable web link for quick access to the full competition details.

- **Unique codes** – I add codes to this list, as soon as I can. They might be on a bottle, crisp packet or neck collar – I type the code straight onto a note, or snap a quick photo. When I've entered the unique code into a draw, I delete it from my note.

- **Tiebreaker entries** – If I enter a story, slogan, caption or poetry competition I copy and paste my entry into this notebook for future reference.

- **Photos of competition details and entry forms** – Evernote uses OCR (optical character recognition) to extract text from photos and make it searchable.

- **List of prize vouchers and gift card expiry dates** – It's easy to forget about a voucher you've won, and incredibly frustrating to find it after it's expired! When I win a voucher, I add it to my list, keeping them in date order, and check regularly to make sure nothing goes to waste – if I realise I can't use a voucher in time, I offer it to friends or in a swaps group.

- **Receipt and barcode photos** – I keep packaging safe until a competition is over, but uploading photos of receipts to Evernote can mean less panicked rummaging if I win. These days most promoters want an emailed receipt rather than a posted one, and you can email it directly from Evernote.

- **Terms and Conditions** – If I'm putting a lot of effort into a competition, I always save a copy of the T&Cs (either copied & pasted or a screenshot) in Evernote, plus a link to the online version. The promoter might change them or delete them, so it's good to have something to refer back to.

Evernote tips

- To make text into a clickable link, highlight it and use Cmd+K (Mac) or Ctrl+K (PC). This is great for saving a list of competitions to do – especially for those long Facebook addresses, as you can simply type 'Boden' and make that word into a link to a Facebook comp.

- Add tags to your files and notes to make them easy to find – *POP, slogan*, etc.

- Evernote assigns you a special unique email address – save this in your contacts, so you can email files directly to Evernote notebooks.

- Set reminders on individual notes –you'll receive an email and a notification in Evernote when it's due (useful for reminding yourself about a competition deadline).

- Install the Evernote *web clipper* browser plug-in to save web pages, photos, links, or a full or partial screenshot of a website.

Find a full list of Evernote shortcuts on their blog at **blog.evernote. com**. If you'd like to start using Evernote, using my referral link will give you a month's free access to Evernote Premium – sign up at **www.superlucky.me/GetEvernote**.

73. Speed up Twitter with Tweetdeck

Tweetdeck is a powerful free tool you can use with your Twitter account(s) – use it to schedule tweets, follow lists, and to search for competitions. Of course, you can use it to enter Twitter comps too!

Sign in at **www.tweetdeck.com** – or download the app to your computer. When you first open it up you might feel rather overwhelmed with information. Tweetdeck shows a column view of your Twitter news feed and notifications, with new tweets automatically scrolling. If it's too much to handle, click the gear icon in the bottom left corner, click on *Settings* and uncheck the *Stream tweets in realtime* option. You can always pause a Tweetdeck column by scrolling down slightly; the column won't start scrolling again until you return to the top.

In your scrolling feed, hover over a tweet to reply, retweet or favourite – or click the **More** (three dots) button to follow a user. Click on the timestamp to open a tweet in a browser window.

Tweetdeck works best when you customise the columns – you can add as many columns as you like. Here are a few suggestions to get you started:

- **Set up searches** to look for prizes on your wishlist, comps in your local area, or the type of comps you like – eg. *'Instagram competition'*, *'Brighton win'* or *'Win weekend break'*.

- **Track a hashtag** – for example *#WinitWednesday*, *#WinningWednesday* or *#FreebieFriday*. Adjust the settings by clicking the top of the column, then going into the *Contents* menu to exclude any retweets, which can clog your feed.

- **View your Twitter lists** – a *Compers* column will give you a constant stream of competitions to enter, or you can subscribe to the **Lucky Learners** members list.

- **Set up a Twitter party column** – type the party hashtag into the search box to track all the action.

- **Experiment with different search terms** to see what you get – *'Facebook competition'* or *'blog giveaway'* will give you links to new non-Twitter promotions too.

Tweetdeck offers lots more in addition to the flexible columns. You can use it to schedule tweets for the future – type in the new tweet box and enter the date and time underneath. The tweet will be sent at that time, even if you don't have Tweetdeck open. This is useful if you want to enter a competition right before it finishes, but know you won't be online. If you like the idea of scheduling tweets, you could also try the free **Hootsuite** app.

74. Download mobile apps

Mobile apps are a popular way to enter competitions and prize draws – as well as downloading social apps like Pinterest, Instagram, Twitter, Messenger, Snapchat, Whatsapp and Facebook, you should also be looking out for new apps for venues, festivals, shops and more. My local shopping centre launched an app last year, and if you used it to share a selfie taken in the centre you could win a £250 prize – it was fiddly to use and in the end I won because I was the *only* valid entrant!

Keep an eye out for mentions of apps in Twitter and Facebook ads and check to see if there are promotions you can enter by downloading to your device. Mobile apps generally aren't the easiest things to get to grips with – I wish more companies considered making YouTube guides on how to use them!

Here are a few of the apps I recommend you should download:

Shazam

Shazam is an app for phones and tablets which identifies music within seconds and tells you what it is. It's brilliant for identifying an old rave anthem playing in a club, a song for an on-air radio competition or the music on an advert. Shazam has a database of more than 11 million songs, and will use your phone's built-in microphone to capture an 'acoustic fingerprint' which it will try to match against a song in that database. If it does, the artist, track and album details are shown on the screen, along with a thumbnail image of the artwork, links to buy and listen to the track and, if relevant, a YouTube video.

Shazam has already been used for several promotions – usually you have to Shazam a track or an advertisement on TV, and then you'll be able to access an entry form via the phone app. It's currently more popular for US promotions, but hopefully we'll see it being used more frequently in the UK – you might spot competitions on Shazam advertising banners too. Keep an eye on **@shazam** on Twitter for news of any promotions, and download the app for free at **www.shazam.com**.

Blippar

Blippar, like the similar app *Aurasma,* is an 'augmented reality' app where you use the camera on your mobile device to scan a product or advert. The screen shows an interactive video or game superimposed on the product, or sometimes a virtual 'scratchcard'. It's usually an instant win mechanism with a daily entry option, and you tap or rub the screen to see if you've won a prize. If you're a lucky winner, an entry form will pop up to take your details. Companies that have used Blippar for prize promotions include Argos, Magners Cider and the UK National Lottery.

Download Blippar for free at **www.blippar.com** and check **www. facebook.com/blippar** for news of promotions.

"I've had great success with the Blippar app – £500 ASOS vouchers by blipping Wrigleys gum, £1,000 Argos vouchers by blipping the catalogue, and I've won three cases of Juiceburst drinks!" – D Adams

---

FutureText

FutureText is a free app for iPhones and iPads. It's not very sophisticated but if you need to send a regular text entry for a competition, or want to send a competition entry on a certain day, it can help. Download the app by searching for it in the App Store. To use it, first add the competition number to your phone contacts list – use the phone number (or short code) as the contact name, eg. 60033.

Open the FutureText app, and select the contact in your list. Next, select the *Date and time* to send the message. Tap *Enter message* and type the text: it might be a simple keyword or full name and address details. Finally, select a *Repeat option* if required (hourly, daily, weekly or monthly). You can add as many FutureText messages as you like.

FutureText works not by sending the text, but by sending you a daily notification. Tap the notification on your screen and the text is there ready to go: you just need to tap send. Unfortunately there's nothing quite clever enough to automatically send the text just yet!

A similar app for Android is **GO SMS Pro** – or search for SMS scheduler in the store for a few options.

Other apps

I blog about the latest apps with prizes at **www.superlucky.me**. I've recently won with the **ASAP54** fashion app, and plenty of my readers have been lucky with the daily draws on the **WAMO** app. If you don't mind taking and uploading photos of your receipts, then download **Shopitize** and **CheckoutSmart** for cashback offers and competitions – I won a beer fridge with CheckoutSmart when I bought a four-pack of Heineken! **Bounts** is a great app if you like to keep track of your exercise – they've given away prizes for sharing your workouts on Twitter.

Tips

- When new apps are launched, it's often in conjunction with a promotion. Try searching Google or Twitter for *'download app win'* or a similar group of search terms.

- Apps take up a lot of space on your device – have a regular clear out of old ones (you can always download again in the future).

- If you win something using an app, take a screenshot of the winning message as proof (you can take a screenshot by holding down the Home key and pressing the power key on an iPhone/ iPad – for other mobile devices the technique varies).

75. Use IFTTT

IFTTT (*"If this, then that"*) is a clever website where you can set up or use 'recipes' online. Nothing to do with cooking, these recipes are ways of automating things. If a certain *trigger* happens, then you tell IFTTT to do an *action*. For example, if a certain user sends a tweet, IFTTT can automatically email that tweet to you.

Before you start dabbling in recipes, however, you'll have create your account at **www.IFTTT.com** and connect a few *channels* such as Twitter and Instagram.

Once you've registered, click *Create Recipe* to get started. First, you need to specify the *'If this...'* part of your recipe – for example, a new result in a Twitter search for *'win holiday to Spain'*. Next, add the *'...then that'* part, for example send an email. So every time there's a new tweet containing the words *'win holiday to Spain'*, IFTTT will send you an email. Here are a few example recipes:

- *If @Boden_Clothing posts a photo on Instagram, email me the link*

- *If I favourite a tweet, add the link to a spreadsheet in my Google Drive folder*

- *If @SuperLuckyDi sends a tweet, email me the link.*

- *Send all tweets with the #SuperLuckySecrets hashtag to a spreadsheet in Drive*

There are lots of other ways IFTTT can be used – browse the recipes on the website to give you a few ideas.

76. Use Unroll.me to control your inbox

The problem with comping is that it rapidly fills up your inbox – if you don't check your emails for a couple of days, it's a nightmare to sort out. I use the **Unroll.me** website to organise my email subscriptions into a single daily digest, and it's a big timesaver.

To use Unroll.me, you will have to give them access to your email address and password. It then scans your inbox to find the lists you're subscribed to. You can choose to unsubscribe, add to a daily email (the *Rollup*) or leave untouched in your inbox. My Rollup includes about 80 emails each day, which I can scroll through quickly to see if there are any good competitions featured – this is far quicker than manually reading and deleting 80 messages in my inbox.

Here's how to use Unroll.me:

- Go to **http://unroll.me** and enter your email address. Read and accept the T&Cs, then input the password for your email account. Current email providers supported are Outlook.com (including Hotmail, MSN, & Windows Live), Gmail, Google Apps, Yahoo! Mail, AOL Mail, and iCloud.

- Unroll.me will then start trawling through your inbox to establish the mailing lists you're on.

- When it's finished, you'll be presented with an alphabetical list of the mailing lists you subscribe to – if you've been comping for a while this could be over a thousand.

- Click to **unsubscribe from email lists**. Note that in some cases, unsubscribe requests fail and instead, Unroll.me will just stop emails from that sender reaching your inbox.

- **Keep emails from senders in your inbox** by leaving them untouched on your Unroll.me list.

- **Add the sender to your Rollup list** to include their emails in a single daily digest.

Once you've set everything up, just wait for the first Rollup to arrive in your inbox. It features neat thumbnails of each email so you can scroll through and click to open the original up (via the Unroll.me site) if you spot anything interesting… such as a competition!

The emails included in the Rollup are also filed into an 'Unroll.me' folder in your email inbox, so you can always access the original emails if you need to – remember to trash the emails in this folder occasionally too.

When you receive your daily Rollup there may be a banner at the top to say *'We found 25 new subscriptions in your inbox. Why not roll them up or unsubscribe?'*. Click it to go to Unroll.me and check the *'New items'* folder, where you can unsubscribe, add these new senders to your Rollup or leave them in your inbox.

I've found Unroll.me to be invaluable – my daily inbox check now takes me a couple of minutes rather than an hour!

77. Store files in Drive or Dropbox

Google Drive and *Dropbox* are both free methods of storing files, photos, videos and documents in the cloud – everything you save is synced automatically to all your devices. You can download the Drive or Dropbox app to your mobile device.

If you're an Instagram user, you've probably encountered that annoying situation where the photo you want to share is on your computer and you need to get it to your mobile phone. If you have Drive/Dropbox open in your browser, you can drag and drop the photo, then open it with the app on your phone. You can also do the reverse – upload to the app from your phone, then access the photos from your computer. Create a new folder in Drive/Dropbox called 'comp photos' and save all your great entries in there (with relevant names) so you can access them at any time.

Dropbox

Dropbox.com is a basic file storage service, offering 2GB storage to new users, with the ability to arrange files into folders and sub-folders. You can share folders with other people, which is handy if a file is too big to send via email – for example a video entry to a competition.

If you refer friends to Dropbox, you can earn 500MB extra storage for each one who joins. If you want to sign up to use Dropbox, you can use my **referral link** which will give me a bonus 500MB storage – thanks!

Drive

Drive.google.com is free and gives you a generous 15 GB of free online storage. Like Dropbox, you can keep photos and videos in folders which can be accessed from anywhere. If you have a gmail address, you will already have Google Drive. Although I use Dropbox for work purposes, my preference as a comper is Drive, as I also use it to create **prize spreadsheets** (tip 88) and store my PDF versions of Compers News magazine.

Finding your wins

Lots of winners miss out on prizes simply because they don't know where to look for winning messages or announcements. Only a small percentage of promoters inform winners by post or telephone now, so you really need to be on the ball when it comes to checking emails and searching for your name online. The tips in this section will help you keep track – and maybe even claim a few missed prizes.

78. Always answer your phone

For online and postal prize draws, lots of promoters still ask for a telephone number because that's how they will be contacting the winners. When you start comping, your phone number is likely to get into the hands of a few annoying companies, simply because of those tempting adverts on Google and competition sites that lead you to the dreaded tick box surveys, where you agree to pass your details on to endless third parties. Unfortunately that's something most compers learn to live with, but we also know that one day that phone will ring and it will be a notification of a huge win!

My tip is to always answer the phone politely, even if you think it's a scam. Promoters have told me of their bad WTC (winning telephone call) experiences where the winner has hung up in anger!

Always answer a *"number withheld"* call – otherwise you'll be left wondering if you missed something amazing. You might be surprised to hear that some promoters only give you one chance to answer the phone, before moving on to call a replacement winner. Lots of them *won't* leave a voicemail message – if the winner is away for a few weeks, and the prize is time-critical (event tickets for example) then the winner will be very disappointed (possibly even angry) when they listen to the message. Don't worry too much though – most decent promoters will try to call you several times before giving up. So turn that volume up and keep your phone handy! If you answer and the caller asks you to confirm your name, don't get too suspicious. There are plenty of comps that require you to simply text one keyword, eg. TICKETS or CAR, so the person calling won't know a thing about you. Several years ago my friend Lorraine answered her comping phone after a couple of missed calls to be greeted with *"Hello, could you confirm your name please?"* – she was taken aback and suspicious, but it turned out she had won a brand new car in a simple text comp!

"I was very hesitant about answering a call from a withheld number. It was a lady from Channel 4, who told me I had won a Toyota Aygo! I'd entered it on the T4 website. I was in shock for hours!" – Vanessa Alvis

---

If you miss a call on your phone and they didn't leave a message, check to see if the number is stored in 'recent calls'. Don't call back straight away – it might be an expensive scam. The first thing you should do is search for the number at **www.google.com**. There are websites where people report the details of nuisance calls from PPI, loan or accident companies. If it turns out your mystery call was from one of those, my advice would be to immediately block the caller from your phone – or save the number on your phone with a description like 'Scam PPI'. Do this by tapping 'i' next to the number (on an iPhone).

If your Google search is more promising and the number belongs to a marketing agency, prize fulfilment company, or the head office of a big brand, call them back. Otherwise you'll be sitting around nervously waiting for another call – which may never come! It's a good idea to have some knowledge of the possible prize though – check any records you might have, or search comping forums for details. When you call back, tell them you think you might have won a competition prize and couldn't resist calling back because you were excited.

Where possible, save the caller in your contacts so you'll see a description if they call again.

79. Search for your name on Facebook

If you enter competitions on Facebook then you're probably aware of the big problem – how on earth do you know if you've won?

Prize draws and comps hosted on Facebook apps are great because they either allow a promoter access to the entrant's registered Facebook email address, or the promoter collects details via an entry form. Winners are emailed and the promoter knows they've done their job in contacting them.

For comps on a Facebook timeline where you simply have to like, share or comment to enter, the promoter has no access to an email address and will attempt to contact a winner using a few unreliable methods. You might see them add a comment to the competition post, announcing all the winners (possibly tagging the names), or they might reply to the individual winner's comments. Sometimes they announce the winner in a brand new post. In most cases they will ask the winner to contact them, either by message or email. Ideally, promoters will send messages to their winners too (see tip 80, **Check your Other messages on Facebook**).

Search posts using Facebook search bar

Some (not all) Facebook members have the ability to search posts, but you'll need to ensure your language is set to English (US) at **www.facebook.com/settings** first. Then in the search bar at the top type your name and add *"congratulations"* or *"winner"*. Select **Posts** to filter the results – you can't view posts in order so it's a bit hit and miss what you end up with, but you may stumble across something exciting.

Search for your name in a winners group

Competition Winners is my public Facebook group where anyone can search to see if they have been announced as a winner in a UK competition or prize draw – without having to join the group. Winning emails, messages, status updates or Facebook notifications are often missed, and the purpose of the group is to help people claim their prizes by sharing these announcements, and where possible members can tag other members or friends who may have missed them.

- Group members share winners lists in various ways – by sharing Facebook posts, copying and pasting posts or comments and taking screenshots of winners lists.

- Group members can 'tag' winners in a post or comment by typing @ and then a name. If they are a group member, a friend or even a friend of a friend, the name will automatically pop up. When a name is tagged they get a Facebook notification, can check the post in Competition Winners and click through to, or search for the promoter's page, to respond.

- Search the group for posts at the top right by typing in your name – this will search any text posted in the group, but not the text in shared links, so you may want to pop in regularly to scroll through the latest announcements. If you use a mobile device, you will need to view the 'desktop' version of the site in your web browser, as there's no search function in the Facebook app.

- If you find a win on the page, it's polite to thank the poster and the tagger by tagging them back.

You can find the group at **www.facebook.com/groups/ CompWinners**. In the USA, the equivalent group is Sweepstakes Winners at **www.facebook.com/groups/SweepWinners** and in Australia it's **Competition Winners Australia.**

"I'm grateful to the members of the Competition Winners group for letting me know if I've won something. I'm sure most people would agree - it doesn't matter if you've already received direct notification from the promoter, being tagged (and congratulated!) as a winner feels just as good!" –
Neill Johnstone

80. Check your Other messages on Facebook

In an ideal world a promoter should always send the winner a message via the Message button on their Facebook profile. The problem is that a Facebook page can *only* send a message to a fan who has already messaged them. In most cases they have to send the message from a personal profile (usually one of the admins from the company page) – and many companies don't like to do this. Sometimes you may get a message from a 'fake' looking account set up to contact winners on behalf of a company – don't be overly suspicious and dismiss it straight away.

Because you're not friends with the account that's contacting you, Facebook will send this message either to your **Other** inbox, or your **Spam** inbox. Annoyingly, you can't get notifications or emails about messages arriving in these folders, so make sure you're regularly checking at **www.facebook.com/messages/other** and **www.facebook.com/messages/spam**. You may also find random messages from odd strangers who *"are very liking your profile picture"*!

On a mobile device, there's no way of accessing the Other and Spam inboxes using the Facebook app, but you can access them in your phone or tablet's web browser – choose the option to **View desktop site** from your browser menu and then zoom in to see your messages.

If you're lucky enough to find a winning message in the Other folder, reply straight away – even if it's from months ago. If the message doesn't state that you need to respond within a certain time to claim your prize, you may still be able to explain your situation to the promoter and receive it. I dread to think how many winning messages are sitting unread in people's Other inboxes!

"I won a Mother's Day competition after seeing it on SuperLucky and the winning notification was in my 'other' inbox. Thankfully I happened to check, as it was for a huge £200 bouquet of flowers in a vase, and they needed to know the address ASAP so it would arrive in time!" – Elizabeth G

---

81. Use Social Searcher

Social Searcher is a website where you can search Facebook, Twitter, Google+, Pinterest, Instagram and Linked In. Use the right search terms and it can track down winning announcements you know nothing about!

Use the *Google Social Search* tool for the best results. Go to **www. social-searcher.com/google-social-search**, type your keywords into the box at the top and click *Search*.

Here are a few suggestions (replace 'Di Coke' or superluckydi with your Facebook name or Twitter name of course!) but there are lots of combinations you can try.

• Congratulations "Di Coke" OR superluckydi OR @superluckydi

• Winner "Di Coke" OR superluckydi OR @superluckydi

The results will appear in columns for each social network you tick – by default they are sorted by *Relevance* but click to change that to *Date*. You'll see your most recent mentions at the top.

Keep in mind that you'll get all sorts of mentions in here, particularly if you like and comment regularly on Facebook, or have a very common name – but hopefully you might spot some wins too.

Social Searcher do offer a paid service where you can get email alerts for your search terms, but I've not found this very effective, and prefer to bookmark the site and do a weekly search.

82. Check your app notifications

Depending on the app you're using, there will be different ways for a promoter to get in contact with you. Make sure you're aware of these – you might want to adjust the settings on your device, so notifiations appear as banners or alerts on your screen.

Pinterest

- A promoter will usually leave a comment on one of your pins with an email address for you to get in touch.

- Click or tap the speech bubble icon, and then choose **You** to access Pinterest notifications.

Instagram

- A promoter may contact you via direct message – a direct mesage must be accompanied by a photo, so they might use your winning photo or a *Congratulations* graphic. Direct messages appear as a dot in the 'in tray' on the Instagram app.

- Alternatively, they may leave a comment on your winning photograph with contact details – this will appear as a number on the speech bubble (notifications) icon.

Facebook

- Facebook notifications can be found by clicking the globe icon – you will probably get a lot! You may get a notification to say that the promoter 'mentioned you in a comment', or that they 'replied to your comment' – or a notification that someone has mentioned you on the winning post, or in a winners group.

Twitter

- On Twitter, look for a number on the envelope icon to show you have a direct message – promoters often message you to let you know you've won, and ask you to respond privately with your details.

- Most promoters will mention you in a tweet too – this will appear as a number on your notifications (the bell icon). If they tweet you and ask you to DM them, go to their page, click the gear icon and *Send a message* – you can only do this if they follow you, although this is supposed to be changing soon.

- It's worth doing a regular Twitter search for your username without the @, and your regular name too – just incase you've not been tagged properly, or a Facebook announcement has been tweeted.

There are many other apps that host competitions, and each one will have a different method of contact. Make sure you know how the winners will be informed before you enter!

83. Search for your name on Google

Google search is excellent for compers – I've already showed you how to search for competitions using the advanced tools, but you should also be regularly searching for your own name in case you've missed a win – my YouTube tutorial at **www.superlucky. me/GoogleYourName** will help you. You'll be surprised how many promoters don't get in touch with their winners and are reliant on you spotting an announcement.

To get started, go to **www.google.com** (log in if you have a Google account) and type *"your name"* – always put your name in quotes, as the results will only include pages with the words in exactly the same order as what's inside the quotes – eg. *"Di Coke"*. For a single word or username, eg. superluckydi, you don't need quotes.

Add a combination of keywords like winner, prize, winners, congratulations, etc. after your name. Type OR in capital letters between search terms, eg. *"Di Coke" winner OR winners OR congratulations* gives results for any of those keywords – without the OR, Google would only show websites that match ALL keywords.

When you get the results, click *Search Tools* (on a mobile device, you'll find this by tapping *More*), change *Any Country* to your country of choice and change *Any Time* to a date range of your choice – try *Past week*.

Name tips

- Try misspelt versions of your name or username – try searching for *"Claire Stephenson"* OR *"Clare Stephenson"*

- If you have the same name as a celebrity, you can exclude words from your search results, simply add a dash (minus sign) before the word eg. *"Chris Martin" -Coldplay* would give you search results on that name, but NOT any that mention Coldplay!

- If you have a common name, consider adding a middle name or initial to your registered Facebook name, eg. *"Sam F Jones"* rather than *"Sam Jones"*. This will make it easier to find your name both on Google, and in Facebook searches – it can be disappointing to claim a prize only to discover that the winner was actually someone else with the same name as you!

When you're happy with your searches – use your **browser bookmarks** to save them for regular visits, or set up **Google Alerts**.

84. Search your email inbox

If you can keep your inbox tidy by filing emails as they arrive, you'll find it easier to keep on top of it. If you leave it to fill up you'll find it overwhelming and hard to spot any important emails.

If your inbox is full, your first job should be to search it for WEMs (winning emails) using keywords like *congratulations, runner up* or *winner*. Using the *Rules* function in your email software, you can choose to highlight, flag or file any incoming message that includes these words. Check for this under Edit, Options or Tools on your menu bar. You may have the option to set audio alerts or pop-up messages, to be sure you don't miss anything that could be an exciting WEM. You will probably get lots of non-WEMs flagged up too, but at least if you do have a *real* one it will be brought to your attention straight away!

As well as searching your inbox, search your spam and junk folders regularly – winning emails can often be found hiding in there.

apologising, but it was too late as they'd already posted it to a runner-up. In the post two days later a set of lingerie arrived with a handwritten note saying 'Sorry you missed out on the full prize'. How kind! So it's always worth trying to chase up a win even if it seems too late... you never know!" – Elizabeth G

---

85. Respond ASAP to a winning notification

Whether you receive it via text message, Twitter, Facebook or email, you should reply to a winning notification as soon as you can. Don't risk falling at the final hurdle by ignoring a *"you have 48 hours to respond with your full postal address"* request. If you're on a phone and can't reply there and then, screenshot the message and deal with it when you do your daily camera roll check (see tip 11, **Make the most of your smartphone**).

It's important to double-check your details when you respond – I've had winners reply with typos in email addresses and letters missing off postcodes, and they wonder why they haven't received their prize! Make sure you set up a comping signature for your email and use keyboard shortcuts to ensure your details are always accurate.

Tips for staying motivated

When you start comping it may be months before you get your first prize, and even compers with years of experience find themselves in the occasional 'dry spell'. This section covers a few ways you can stay enthusiastic about the hobby.

86. Be inspired by other winners

It's hard not to feel jealous of other compers when you're struggling to get your first decent win, but following their lead and being inspired by their efforts and prizes will help you be more successful. Take time out to congratulate others on their wins too – I've seen some glorious Facebook posts where people have won their first trip abroad, or a prize from their wish list. All these magical moments will remind you why the hobby is so very special!

On the SuperLucky blog I make the effort not only to share my own successes but also those of my blog readers. In the *Inspiration* section of the blog you'll find:

- **'Win Some Lose Some' posts** – at the end of each year I look back at my comping successes and favourite failures.

- **SuperLucky Stories** – an annual series of posts featuring fun prizewinning entries from SuperLucky readers.

- **Meet the Compers** – interviews with successful and creative compers all over the world.

"I read every part of the Meet the Compers feature on the blog and they all inspired me in different ways. I was inspired by Paul making wings from Post-It Notes, and shared the idea with my husband because I am always trying to get him more involved with creative competitions. We entered and won the September Post-It Notes competition and received £1,500 – our biggest win ever!" – Dawn F

87. Look at your prize scrapbook

It's a great idea to save your winning letters, emails and photos in a prize folder – I love A4 transparent files from Muji and have filled four of them up so far.

Back in the day, when every prize notification arrived hand-delivered by the postman, filling a prize folder was a lot easier. The *'Long White Envelope'* was opened with glee and the letter filed away, perhaps along with the entry form or original competition details too. Now the majority of comps appear online, and notification of a win comes by email or tweet, so the postman rarely brings those LWEs. I still print out screenshots of instant wins and congratulations emails for my folder though – sometimes even Facebook posts!

If you're living your life online, you can still create a virtual 'folder' there too. Taking photos of prize deliveries and screenshots of winning announcements is a great idea and so easy to do if you have a smartphone. Share snaps on Instagram or Twitter, or create a Facebook photo album of prizes – you can even invent your own hashtag to track the photos. If you don't want to share your successes with the world, create a private Facebook album of prize photos by changing the privacy setting to 'only me'.

Browsing through your wins can be a great motivation during those dreaded dry spells, to remind you of the joy comping can bring. I always chuckle at my appearances on the front page of the Nottingham Topper and Loughborough Trader newspapers!

"Thanks to comping I have been able to take my children to Barcelona for a long weekend to watch the football, won a week's holiday in Newquay, taken my husband to New York, Guernsey and St. Ives, and am looking forward to going to Disneyland Paris and Alton Towers. I was able to give both of my sons brand new iPads and so many other gifts and gadgets that we would have never ever been able to afford. It's the buzz of seeing someone smile because something you did has given them something they love!" –
Carrie Talbot-Ashby

88. Create a spreadsheet of success

It's a bit geeky, but I'm a big fan of data, sums and statistics. I enjoy tracking my prizes, their value and the type of competitions I win them in. It's fascinating to monitor where successes are coming from, and I can adjust my comping schedule to suit.

Since 2011 I've saved my prize lists using Google Drive, which you can set up at **drive.google.com**. You'll need a Google or Gmail account to do this. Use the Drive mobile app too, and you can access and add to your spreadsheet from your computer, phone or anywhere in the world – it's much more flexible than keeping a list in just one place.

Keeping a spreadsheet of wins can be really useful in lots of ways:

• See which type of competitions you're most successful with.

• Calculate the value of the prizes you win over a certain period of time.

• Keep track of the prizes you've not yet received and the date you won them, so you don't forget to chase them up.

- Motivate yourself in a dry spell – you'd be amazed how many small prizes you win, and making sure you list *all* of them makes you feel more positive.

- At a glance you can see which prize came from which promoter, so you can thank them for it.

Set up a Google Drive Spreadsheet

Register with Google – if you use a Gmail address you'll already have done this. Log in at **drive.google.com** and click *new* to start a new sheet. Across the top, add column headings:

- **Prize** – what you won.

- **Promoter** – the company, blog or magazine you won with.

- **Value** – so you can total up prize value for the year.

- **Media** – for example, Facebook or radio.

- **Type of comp** – for example, photo or text entry.

- **Won** – the date you won (I like to use a reverse format for this, eg. 15.06.23 rather than 23.06.15, so that if I sort that column into A>Z order, it will also appear in date order).

- **Responded** – the date you replied to the winning email, tweet, etc with your details.

- **Received** – the date you received the prize.

- **Thanked** – complete this box when you've said thank you (either privately or with a public photo or tweet).

- **Notes** – add expiry dates for vouchers, or other notes.

To see the running total of your wins, click *value* to select that column and look for the sum in the bottom corner of your spreadsheet. At the end of the year I guarantee you'll be surprised at how the wins add up!

"I'm running a win list spreadsheet, and thus freeing up acres of brain space that was previously devoted to trying to remember who to chase when!" – Neill Johnstone

89. Celebrate your wins

Don't be shy. If you've won something amazing be sure to tell everyone you know – enjoy your moment in the spotlight, you'll remember it for years to come. Don't worry about any jealous haters – just let them know that your prizes come from dedication and suggest they get stuck in too!

I was on my way to New Zealand when I found out I'd won my VW Beetle, and my friend Sarah posted about my win on the Compers News Chatterbox forum. When I returned from my trip I read through almost a hundred congratulations posts and printed them off for my wins file – it's a wonderful experience to share your wins with other people!

If you're a subscriber to a magazine like Compers News or Simply Prizes, you can win cash or vouchers for your winning stories and photos. Writing about the elation you felt when you received a winning telephone call, or your dream trip to Hawaii, will keep you motivated and get you keen to win another prize. If you win a prize from a magazine, write a letter to them about it: you may well get another prize in return!

"SuperLucky is my first port-of-call when I'm looking for a creative competition or some comping inspiration. I think Di has done a wonderful thing in fostering a comping community in which people are genuinely happy for each other's successes." – Laura G

Don't even think about it!

I've given you lots of tips on what you *should* be doing to ensure you get the best out of your comping hobby – and here are my suggestions of what *not* to do.

90. Don't enter a comp you're not sure is genuine

When you start entering competitions, hopefully it won't be long before you receive genuine winning emails and letters. These will be addressed to you by name and usually signed off by another real person. Unfortunately, you may also receive dodgy correspondence – ranging from letters informing you that you could be in with a chance of winning £100,000, to emails stating you've won an iPad but need to send somebody money to post it from America. You might receive a phone call claiming you've won a fabulous holiday which is actually a week's self-catering accommodation for one person, with no flights included.

If you're not sure if something is legitimate, try searching for the company name, web address or phone number on Google. There are many helpful sites where people post up their experiences with scams and spam. You can also check who owns a website at **www. whois.com**.

Facebook

Compers are the ideal target for a scam Facebook page. Prizes of DisneyWorld tickets or BMWs seem too good to be true, and that's because they usually are. Running *'Like & Share'* scams on Facebook is known as *'Like-Farming'*, and it works because pages with hundreds of thousands of fans are valuable. When these fake posts are liked, shared and commented on by Facebook users and their friends, the pages rapidly gain Likes. The pages are sold and used to send out spam advertising to the fan base, and in some cases they share links directing fans to sign up for expensive text messaging services.

There are several clues to help you spot a Facebook scam:

- Check the **About** tab – if there's no website listed, or the linked site bears no relevance to the Facebook page, be suspicious. Ask yourself, what's the point of their page if there's no linked site?

- If there are a huge number of desirable prizes – a hundred iPads, or five cars for example – it's a scam. Genuine promoters don't give away valuable prizes like these via *like & share* timeline promotions – they use a Facebook app to capture data from the entrants.

- Spelling mistakes or a full stop in the page name or prize description are a clue to the fakes – for example iPhone and iPad always have a lower case i and upper case P in the names.

- Does the page name include a big brand (eg. Argos, Tesco, Apple etc.) *without* a blue tick next to the company name? The blue tick shows it's an official page – note, there is no official Apple page on Facebook.

- The promotion has no terms and conditions or closing date.

- The page has only been set up recently.

If you're not sure a comp is genuine, DON'T enter it. Ask for advice on a comping forum or Facebook group, or check **www. hoax-slayer.com** to see if the scam appears there. Never give your bank details – there's a rare occasion where a promoter may ask if they can do a bank transfer when you win, but make sure you trust that company before giving them your account details.

My advice is to only enter competitions directly on the website, Facebook page or Twitter page of a company you trust, and make sure you have up to date anti-virus software on your computer.

91. Don't allow your details to be passed to third parties

Surveys and tick boxes are the bane of a comper's life. Once you've got to grips with the hobby, you'll understand that most tick boxes should be treated with contempt. Read the small print carefully to check what you're opting in to or out of – some boxes will be pre-ticked, some boxes will require a tick. Opt out of any further correspondence unless it's a company you trust – choosing to receive no further communication will make *no* difference to your chance of being picked as a winner. If you *have* to agree to receive further information in order to enter, consider whether you really want to do so.

So, why is it that new compers are so quick to tick the boxes? When they start comping, Google searches and ads will attract them to sites like My Offers with their huge prizes of £5,000 vouchers, cars and dream holidays. Despite what people say, My Offers isn't a scam. They *do* give away prizes – but the chance of winning is miniscule, because they advertise so widely and have hundreds of thousands of people entering each draw. Entering a prize draw on My Offers means your personal details will be forwarded on to lots of other companies who will spam you like crazy – so don't be tempted!

If you're wondering which other UK websites to avoid, start with *UKPrize, PrizeStore, GetMeATicket, Catalink, Topfox, OffersClick, Surveys, PrizeReactor* and *OfferX* – and check **www.superlucky.me/ CompetitionWebsites** for an up-to-date list. All these sites require you to receive further information and will generate emails, post and phone calls from loan companies, double glazing firms, insurance companies, etc. The prizes on these websites are real, but your chance of winning is tiny so in my opinion it's not worth entering.

If you use **www.ThePrizeFinder.com**, you'll see that the top competitions listed will be from these spam-generating sites – once you learn to spot and skip those listings, you'll find the website much more useful.

92. Don't waste time tracking entries

Some compers jot down details of every competition they enter, or keep a spreadsheet of entries online. I think it's madness – the ratio of losing entries to winning ones would have a dreadful effect on a comper's spirit!

Using the tracker function on a website like The PrizeFinder or Loquax is quicker, but in my opinion it's still a waste of valuable comping time. People tell me they use trackers so they don't enter the same competition or prize draw twice – but from experience, I know that most decent promoters don't mind. They will simply give you a single entry in the draw and ignore any further entries you've made – it would have to be a rather mean promoter to completely disqualify you. Sometimes you'll get a little *'Oops, looks like you've already entered'* message.

With Facebook and Twitter prize draws, you can only like a post or retweet once, so there's no danger of you entering twice, and most compers do tend to remember if they've already visited an online entry form. If you like competition listings sites, then just stick to using one of them – that cuts down the risk of entering twice.

Some compers like to track competitions so they know what the prize is or which promoter it was from – but in most cases if you win, you can Google to find a record of the competition online (Money Saving Expert is useful for this).

I use **Evernote** to keep a very limited list of my competition entries. The only ones I add are creative competitions where I've put effort in, where I want to be sure the winner is chosen according to the T&Cs. I check this list every few weeks and chase up any comps where there has been no winner announced.

Tracking your wins, on the other hand, is *definitely* worth doing – everyone should create a **spreadsheet of success** (tip 88)!

93. Don't enter voting competitions

Many of the readers of this book will have had success in a voting competition – and I'll admit that I have too – but my advice would be to steer clear. They are time-consuming, fraught with stress and rarely run in a fair manner – and prize promotion specialists the *Institute of Promotional Marketing*, *PromoVeritas* and *Spark & Fuse* agree.

There are many reasons a voting competition doesn't work:

- **Fans won't vote** unless incentivised by a prize, and even then most won't bother.The only people who vote are friends of the entrant (usually begrudgingly), compers (when they've been asked), people who are paid to vote, and vote-exchangers who need a return vote.

- **People can easily buy and swap votes worldwide** – either by paying a minimal amount for votes from real people, or exchanging votes from fake Facebook accounts. Some entrants even add votes to their competitors' entries to try and get them disqualified!

- **The best entry rarely wins.** To get round this, promoters might put a judged shortlist to the vote. But even from a shortlist the most deserving entry rarely wins, it will usually be the entrant with the most time, friends and sly methods of getting votes.

- **People will cheat.** If it's a photo or recipe competition decided solely on votes, cheats will Google for entries to submit. They will enter under lots of different names, and are probably vote-exchanging.

- **They are a PR disaster.** People love to moan about voting competitions, and usually it's in public. They'll moan about the cheating, the plagiarism, the compers, and that it's a 'popularity contest'.

If you spot a voting competition and aren't happy about it, try contacting the promoter with your concerns (and perhaps a link to my blog post on the horrors of voting at **http://bit.ly/VoteCompsSuck**) and ask them to reconsider the voting element. A surprising percentage of promoters do listen and reconsider the format – if not this time, then certainly next time round. It's rare for a company to run a voting competition more than once!

You might see a competition where every entry with a certain number of votes (around 15 is achievable and reasonable) is put into a random draw, or judged – this is about the only fair way to run a voting competition. The promoter still achieves viral sharing without spamming. I won a once-in-a-lifetime luxury football trip to Milan in an Indesit competition where you needed 20 votes to qualify – once you achieved those votes, entries were judged on creativity and passion for football. That seems fair to me!

If you do get involved with a voting competition, be prepared for the bitching and trolling that comes with it. Accusations will fly, people will get upset and, if you come out as the winner, it will feel like a hollow victory, with people convinced you didn't deserve to win.

94. Don't get carried away with premium rate phone calls and texts

I'm not a fan of promotions where you have to make a costly phone call to enter the draw, although some of my comping friends *have* had big cash wins in phone comps. I prefer to have something physical to show for my spending!

Most competition phone calls cost between £1.50 and £2.00, and are only worth doing if there's no free entry option. Check the terms and conditions carefully – in many cases you will be able to enter via a website or by sending a postcard with your details on (although with the rapid increase in stamp cost, a postcard will soon cost the same as a premium rate phone call!). If there are no other entry methods, and it's a valuable prize you'd really like, then go for it, but check the T&Cs carefully for the exact cost of phone calls. In July 2015 new charges were introduced, with mobile calls now much more expensive than landlines for premium rate numbers due to high 'access rates'. Be careful, a lot of companies and radio stations will try to tempt you by texting back a *'Buy 2 get 1 free'* deal to encourage you to make a second entry! Also beware of text comps advertised in local papers or on local radio – they might actually be hosted across nationwide media, meaning a slim chance of winning. Only spend what you can afford – you might prefer to use a separate SIM card and old phone handset so you can monitor what you spend on the calls.

For promotions advertised in-store and on-pack, the cost of a call or text will usually be standard rate or free – sometimes the standard rate ones will be covered in your monthly allowance.

Finally, never call to claim a prize from a scratchcard you got in a magazine. It will cost you around £10 – check the small print, there will be a postal method that will only cost you the price of a stamp. Be prepared to be disappointed though – you're likely to win a holiday for one (with no travel)!

95. Don't lie

Be careful if you decide to bend the truth. Exaggeration is okay – and can be hilariously funny – but lying about your name, your age, your passport details or your health problems is a bad idea and can come back to haunt you.

Fake names

For all sorts of reasons, people might decide to use a false name to enter competitions, but what happens if the promoter wants to see ID before awarding the prize? A new comper contacted me on Facebook, distraught because she was unable to claim a £500 cash win with Pepsi – she had a completely different name on Facebook to the one on her passport. Pepsi were unsympathetic and she lost out on the prize. Facebook do actually state in their terms of use that you *must* use your real name on your account. Twitter, on the other hand, allow you to remain anonymous and no real names need to be shared. Of course, that's great for shy compers, but unfortunately it also means an easy way for cheats to enter from several accounts simultaneously. My recommendation is to stay safe by using your real name on Facebook and Twitter.

Kids' competitions

If you want to enter competitions to win kids' prizes, check the rules carefully. In most cases it's fine for an adult to enter on behalf of their child – but check if you should be entering with their name or your name. Don't think it's okay to enter with your own name and a child's date of birth – the prize may be withdrawn, which is what happened with Nickelodeon's £6,000 Christmas giveaway. Be careful how much assistance you give for art competitions too – if your child doesn't like colouring in, then don't do it for them. My son doesn't really like colouring-in, and it's something that I've learnt to live with – there are plenty of other activities he enjoys.

Age

Don't lie about your age – there are competitions with strict age guidelines (usually for under 18s or over 50s). Other comps might not state limits, but from the nature of the promoter or prize you can deduce what age they are aimed at and let your morals decide whether to enter.

Telling untruths in a tiebreaker or comment competition is a bad idea – if you don't have a story to tell, perhaps you should skip that competition and enter one that you're enthusiastic about. In my early days of comping I got myself in a pickle when I won a £2,000 cash prize with a last-minute rhyming slogan about a dream honeymoon – at the cheque presentation they kept asking where I would be going, but I wasn't even engaged at the time. I got flustered and bluffed my way out of it, but promised myself I wouldn't risk a lie again, just for the sake of a good rhyme!

96. Don't tell sob stories

You'll see sob stories all the time in Facebook comments. At least on Twitter, the 140 character limit means people can't go into great detail about their recent divorce, lack of carpet in the lounge or their cat's leg operation! But Facebook competition posts can prove depressing reading, and sometimes give us far too much insight into people's personal lives.

Sob stories don't win prizes. Most of us have something awful going on at some point in our lives, and yes, they do say a problem shared is a problem halved. But put yourself in the promoter's shoes here – if they choose a sob story as a winner, it will bring everybody down. Companies run promotions on their Facebook pages to lift people's spirits and give somebody a little treat – and sharing a winning sob story would be a risky thing for a promoter to do.

If you genuinely think it's appropriate to share a sad story, then try to put a positive spin on it. Perhaps a friend is very ill, but she would love to take up a new hobby? Rather than focusing on the negative side of a story, focus on the positives that the prize could bring to their life.

97. Don't be afraid to complain

Unfortunately, in the world of comping, things don't always run smoothly. Promoters make mistakes, people try to cheat and prizes may not be what they seem. With social media so widely used, complaining is easier and more effective than it used to be. In most cases, you can contact promoters on Twitter or Facebook – complaints are usually dealt with swiftly, and most promoters will work to get things fixed. If it's a promotion that's still running, you may be worried about jeopardising your chances by complaining – perhaps you could ask a comping friend to complain on your behalf?

If you're frustrated by unfair competitions then you might want to refer promoters to two of my popular blog posts:

- 10 Reasons why voting comps are a bad idea – **http://bit.ly/ VoteCompsSuck**

- Why your 'Like and Share' promotion isn't fair – **http://bit. ly/ShareUnfair**

If you have cause for complaint, your first step should be a polite private message or email. If you don't get a satisfactory response, you could try a public comment or tweet to the promoter. If they're still not acknowledging your complaint, in the UK you can submit a formal complaint via the Advertising Standards Authority (ASA).

The ASA makes sure all advertising is legal, decent, honest and truthful. All prize promotions must comply with the *The UK Code of Non-broadcast Advertising, Sales Promotion and Direct Marketing* (CAP Code). If you believe a promotion is in breach of the CAP Code, you can complain.

Most people aren't actually aware of what you can complain about – here are a few CAP Code elements you should be aware of:

- Promoters must tell you the winner's name and county – this doesn't need to be public, they can tell you in a private conversation or letter.

- Promoters cannot change the closing date of a competition or prize draw (unless circumstances outside the reasonable control of the promoter make it unavoidable).

- Promoters must not ask a winner to respond by a specified time or date if they need not (exceptions are for time-critical prizes such as event tickets).

- Promoters must make full T&Cs accessible throughout the promotion – entrants should be able to read them all before deciding whether to take part.

- Prize draw winners must be chosen by a verifiably random process.

- Competition winners must be chosen according to a set criteria, and the panel should include at least one independent judge.

Example complaints might be a fake winner, a winning photo that didn't belong to the entrant (use Google's reverse image search at **www.google.co.uk/imghp** to prove this), a prize that didn't materialise, or a voting competition where the winner cheated.

You might find a link to the Sales Promotions section of the CAP Code useful if you're communicating with a promoter who doesn't know the rules – you can find it at **http://bit.ly/CAPCodePromotions**.

The most common complaint I see on social media is the lack of a winning announcement. Entrants don't like to chase up promoters, for fear of jeopardising their chances – the best way to do it is by working as a team with your comping friends. If one of your friends *didn't* enter that particular comp, ask them to politely enquire when the winner will be announced.

Make a formal ASA complaint

The earlier you make a complaint, the more likely it is that the ASA can act while the promotion is still live – be sure to submit your complaint within three months of the advertising appearing. Collect everything you can to help with the investigation, including links, screenshots, T&Cs or photos of promotional materials.

Submit your complaint on the *Make a Complaint* page at **www.asa. org.uk**. Possible categories could be:

- **Internet > Promotions & special offers**
- **Press > National press, Regional press & Magazines**
- **Other > Leaflet, Packaging or Point of Sale**

Upload up to three files by clicking Choose file, browse for your screenshots/scans then click Upload. Add in a website link for the promotion if it's still available. Say where and when you saw the promotion, who the advertiser is, and the product being advertised (the product is the competition or prize draw). Next, add a detailed description of your complaint. The box on the ASA page is small so you might want to type your complaint in Word or a Notes file first, then copy and paste it onto the website. Click on any step to go back and edit before clicking Submit.

When the ASA receives your submission, they will let you know if they take up your complaint. The ASA may be able to resolve the complaint quickly by contacting the promoter, rather than conducting a formal investigation – for example, they could chase up an undelivered prize. Formal investigations take longer. The advertiser will be contacted and asked to provide evidence, the ASA Council will decide whether or not the CAP Code has been breached, and a ruling of *Upheld* (the ASA agrees with you) or *Not Upheld* (the ASA disagrees and no further action will be taken) will be published on the ASA website.

Rulings are published on the ASA website every week and in some cases the national press have picked up on stories of promotions gone bad. If the rules have been breached, the advertisement must be changed or withdrawn. This rarely occurs with prize promotions as by the time an investigation is conducted, the promotion is usually over. Persistent offenders may be referred to Trading Standards or Ofcom for further action.

Unfortunately, the ASA doesn't have any enforcement power, so a ruling against the promoter is often the best you can expect. You may be disappointed with this, but in theory the promoter should learn from their mistakes and get things right next time round. If you can get your complaint in while the promotion is live, you have a better chance of changing things. Where the winner hasn't complied with T&Cs, ASA involvement has been enough for promoters like Santander and Harrods to award another prize to a second winner.

98. Don't forget to say 'thank you'!

When you are lucky enough to win (and you will!), make sure you thank the promoter for your prize. This can be privately by email, letter, Facebook message or Twitter DM, or you can share a public tweet, Instagram photo or Facebook post – the promoter will prefer this as everyone loves to see a happy and genuine winner. You'd be surprised how many winners don't bother to say thanks when they receive a prize, which can be disheartening for the promoter. It's common courtesy to say thank you and if the promoter can see their prize was appreciated, that should encourage them to run more competitions. I've even been known to send holiday postcards to promoters to let them know what a fantastic time I'm having!

As a blogger myself, I'd like to add that it's particularly important to thank a blogger when your prize arrives – mainly because bloggers have no idea when their sponsor has actually posted the prize out. It will take a weight off the blogger's mind to know that the prize has been received safely.

99. Don't enter for prizes you don't want

It makes sense to focus on the prizes you want to win. Unfortunately, a few compers get carried away and enter every giveaway that crosses their path, regardless of the prize. These compers have lofts and garages full of prizes they don't want and can't sell – promotional caps, cuddly toys and posters. Before you enter a comp, take a moment to think – do you want the prize? If not, would a family member or friend like it – or could you donate it as a raffle prize or to a local charity? I feel sad to see beautiful clothes and shoes posted on Facebook selling pages almost as soon as they've been won – and when I win tickets to events there's a surprising number of winners who simply don't show up, rather than letting the promoter know they can't make it. Check the dates and small print before entering – if you can't go, don't enter. If the winners can't even be bothered to turn up, that promoter might not run another comp – and that would be a real shame.

Even if you focus on winning the things you or your family want, you can still end up with plenty of random things – runners-up prizes can be completely unrelated to the main prize you entered for. And of course, even when you *do* win that dream prize – an iPhone, or a pair of designer shoes – the specifications might not be exactly what you expected. Unless it states in the terms and conditions that you can't sell on the prize, it's certainly an option for you to do so.

Everyone has an opinion about compers selling prizes – but keep in mind that entering giveaways for the sole purpose of selling the prize can be insulting to the promoter and other entrants. Whatever you choose to do though – it's *your* prize, so don't feel guilty about it!

Here are a few selling tips:

- Selling items on to family and friends at a bargain price – or asking a favour in return for a freebie – is a great idea.

- You might find a swaps forum on the competition site you use – or you could search for one on Facebook. Ask your comping friends if they know of one.

- There are lots of swaps groups for local areas, and you could consider a nationwide listing on eBay, Gumtree, Preloved or Amazon.

- If you're selling electrical prizes, the promoter won't usually include a receipt. You should still be able to register for a guarantee online – you may have to do this within 30 days of receipt, so do it before you attempt to sell the prize on. You can also sell items with a copy of the prizewinner's letter to show where they came from.

- Other compers will be selling prizes too, and you can pick up some great bargains – I bought a £500 Homebase gift card for £300 from a fellow comper which saved me a fortune on furniture when I moved house. An eBay search on 'unexpected prize' or 'unwanted prize' may give good results too.

" I focus on competitions that I want to win rather than just entering everything in sight. I learned this lesson the hard way when I won a tin of horse cough mixture!" –
Michael Scoates

---

100. Don't give up

Like many, you might get stuck in to comping and then lose heart after a few weeks if your wins total a big fat zero. But this is a hobby where you have to be patient – there *are* a few comps where you find out instantly if you've won, but in most cases winners won't find out until a month or so after entering. Don't give up hope! Join an online forum, comp club or Facebook group to keep yourself motivated. Remember that comping should be an enjoyable hobby and the prizes are a bonus.

If you've been comping for years and haven't been lucky for a while, we call that a *'dry spell'*. Losing your comping mojo isn't unusual, and it happens to most long-term compers at least a couple of times. A new hobby or a life-changing event like a wedding or baby comes along and suddenly you don't have that spare time to dedicate to your comps.

Here's a few ways you can stay enthusiastic:

- Update your wish list and get searching. Spend a few hours dreaming about the prizes – then get searching for them.

- Get out and about – stop shopping online and get yourself to the High Street and supermarket – keep a look out for entry forms, promotional products and magazines.

- Look through your wins folder or spreadsheet to remind yourself what a great hobby you have.

- Find or start a local comp club or Facebook group to find motivated friends.

- If you've been entering the same type of easy prize draws, try something more challenging like searching for low entry comps, or learning to use Instagram.

You *will* start winning again, it's just a matter of time!

"I was bored entering prize draw after prize draw and probably would have given up comping had I not taken Di's advice to make an effort with my entries and look for low entry comps!" – Viv

---

Glossary of comping terms

A list of terms you might encounter in the world of comping.

Advents – Daily prize promotions which begin on 1st December and usually run for 24 days, with 24 prizes. Some companies run *12 days of Christmas* promotions instead.

AIOE – *All In One Envelope*. A method of entering postal prize promotions, where postcards for different competitions can be sent to the same address in a single stamped envelope.

Apps – An abbreviation of *applications*, apps are usually downloaded to a computer or mobile device but you can also add apps to a social media platform such as Facebook or Twitter.

ASA – *Advertising Standards Authority*. The ASA ensure that all UK marketing communications follow the *CAP Code*. Rulings are published weekly at **www.asa.org.uk**, and often include unfair prize promotions.

Aurasma – A free AR (Augmented Reality) app for smartphones and tablets, used to scan products or printed materials.

Autofill/autocomplete – The autofill function is included in most browsers. You can complete name, address, phone and other details in your profile and then click to automatically fill out online entry forms.

Automated entry service – A company that charges people to be entered into competitions and prize draws.

Blippar – A free AR (Augmented Reality) app for smartphones and tablets, used to scan products or printed materials.

Bookmarks – Bookmarks are used in browsers to save and access favourite sites quickly.

Browser – The application used to access the internet, either on a computer or mobile device. The most common are Google Chrome, Safari, Firefox and Internet Explorer.

Bulk entries – A large quantities of entries sent from the same source, eg. from *automated entry services*.

CAP – *Committee of Advertising Practice.*

CAP Code – *The UK Code of Non-broadcast Advertising, Sales Promotion and Direct Marketing.* All prize promotions in the UK must follow the CAP Code, which is enforced by the *ASA*.

Chatterbox/CB – Online forum for *Compers News* members.

Clean link – Some promotions offer bonus entries for referring friends, and after taking part the entrant is given a unique link to share with friends. Every friend who clicks the link and goes on to enter gets the sharer another entry in the draw. In this type of prize draw, a *clean link* is a direct link to the prize promotion. A *dirty link* is where an entrant shares their unique link on a forum, Facebook group or website without telling people they benefit from the click-throughs.

Click to win/C2W/CTW – Easy daily entry prize draws featured on a large number of UK websites owned by Bauer Media – find them all at **winit.winsomething.co.uk.**

Comper – A person who spends time comping. Also see *contestor* or *sweeper*.

Compers News – UK-based monthly subscription-only competition listings magazine published by Accolade.

Competition – In the UK, a competition is a prize promotion where there's an element of skill involved. The winner could be judged or decided by a public vote. Promotions that involve a significant amount of effort to enter – for example a crossword or quiz – are competitions, even if the winner is chosen at random from all correct entries.

Comping – the hobby of entering competitions and prize draws.

Contest – US term for a *competition*.

Contestor – US term for *comper.*

Dailies – Any prize promotion which can be entered daily; there may or may not be a prize to be won each day.

DM – *Direct Message.* Private messages sent on Twitter or Instagram are known as DMs. A promoter might ask you to DM your address if you're a winner. On Twitter, send a DM by clicking the envelope icon, on Instagram look for the in-tray icon. See also *PM.*

Dirty link – See *Clean Link.*

Disqus – A blog comment hosting service.

Entry form – Entry forms can be printed onto leaflets, in magazines or found online on websites or Facebook.

EOM – *End of Month.* Compers are often snowed under with EOM closing dates.

Experiential – *Experiential marketing* creates a bond between the consumer and the brand by immersing them in a fun and memorable experience such as a treasure hunt, often including the chance to win prizes.

Facebook – A social network where individuals connect with friends, set up *profiles* and *groups*, and brands set up *pages* to connect with fans.

Favourites – Using *Favourites* (or *Favorites,* depending where you are and which app you're using!) you can bookmark tweets, Facebook pages, lists and groups for quick reference.

Gleam – An app used to run a prize draw/sweepstakes, usually on a blog.

Handling House – A company that handles the entries to a competition or prize draw.

Hootsuite – A social media management system, where you can schedule tweets and Facebook posts.

IFTTT – An online automation tool, this means *If This, Then That.*

Independent judge – According to the *CAP Code*, winner selection in the UK should be supervised by at least one independent judge who has no connection to the promoter or agency hosting the competition or prize draw.

Instant win – In an *instant win* promotion you find out immediately if you're a winner. This could be via a text message, on-screen message, scratch card or email.

Instant lose – A term used by compers to describe an instant win promotion where the winning codes are pre-decided, and the likelihood of someone entering a winning code from a packet is miniscule.

IPM – The *Institute of Promotional Marketing* is the leading professional body for the UK promotional marketing industry.

Like and Share – The most common type of Facebook promotion. To enter, you simply need to click the thumbs up icon to *Like* the post or photo, then click *Share* and choose the Public option before posting it to your own timeline.

LCC – *London Competitors' Club.*

Loquax – The UK's oldest prize and competition portal, *Loquax* offers bingo, games and a chat forum at **www.loquax.co.uk**.

Loquat – a *Loquax* member

LWE – A *Long White Envelope*. Before the days of social media, most competitions were postal entry and the winners would always be informed by a letter on headed paper, in a long, white, DL-size envelope.

MSE – *Money Saving Expert*. A British consumer finance information and discussion website, which has a forum dedicated to competitions.

News Feed – A Twitter or Facebook *news feed* shows posts from the people and brands you follow.

NPN (No Purchase Necessary) – For some on-pack promotions, or comps in magazines, there may be an NPN route in the T&Cs. You don't need to buy a magazine or product to enter – usually you email or send an SAE for an entry code. In Northern Ireland the law is different to Great Britain, and many purchase-necessary comps will have an NPN entry route for NI.

Offerpop – An application used to run prize promotions, mainly on Facebook.

Other inbox/other messages – Facebook messages that aren't from friends will usually land in either the *Other* or *Spam* inbox. Promoters will ask winners to check their other inbox for a message – it can be accessed at **www.facebook.com/messages/other**.

PIN Code – See *URN*.

PIS – *Post In-Store*. Some venues still have a box for entry forms in-store – you'll sometimes find cheeky compers asking if anyone can *'do a PIS'* for them!

Plain paper entry – A plain paper entry was a popular way to submit an entry for a purchase-necessary promotion in the UK – back when a free entry option was required by law (free entry routes must still be offered to Northern Ireland residents). Entrants should print their name and address details on plain paper and post in an envelope.

PM – A *Private Message* can be sent on Facebook or on an online forum. It won't be seen by anyone except the recipient. See also *DM (Direct Message)*.

Postcard draw – A postcard draw is where the entry must be posted on a stamped postcard – usually a picture postcard, but it can be a blank card.

POP – *Proof Of Purchase*. Something that proves to the promoter that you purchased the product – a bottle cap, receipt (traditional or emailed), barcode, packet, etc.

POS – *Point Of Sale*. This refers to advertising which is seen in shops, venues and restaurants. It could be posters, banners, shelf talkers, leaflets, etc.

Prize draw – A draw where the winner is chosen at random from all valid entries.

PrizeFinder – The UK's biggest free competition listings site.

Quallie/qualifier – A promotional product which needs to be purchased in order to enter a competition or prize draw. It's usually accompanied by a POP. At competition clubs members will usually take a quallie and POP, for example a bottle of wine and a receipt.

Rafflecopter – An app used to run a prize draw/sweepstakes, usually on a blog.

Random.org – A website that chooses a random number from a defined range, suitable for choosing prize draw winners.

Regram/Repost – to share another user's post on your own Instagram feed, usually tagging or crediting the original photographer.

RoboForm – A password management and form-filling programme.

RT – *Retweet*. On Twitter, the act of retweeting shares someone else's tweet on your own timeline. *RT & Follow* is the preferred method of Twitter prize draw.

Share – *Sharing* usually refers to Facebook posts, which can be shared on your own timeline (appearing in your friends' news feeds) or shared on a friend's wall.

Shazam – A music identification app.

Shelf talker – A sign attached to a supermarket shelf, sometimes with a pad of entry forms or a tiny set of T&Cs for a promotion.

Short code – A five-digit number used in the UK for text competitions.

Simply Prizes – A monthly UK prize draw and competition listings magazine published by Oxfordshire Press.

Slogan – A *slogan* competition usually has a set word limit. The entrant sometimes has to complete a sentence.

SMS – *Short Message Service*. See *text message*.

Sweeper – US term for *comper*.

Sweepstakes/Sweeps – US term for a prize draw, with winners chosen at random from all entries.

Tag – A way to mention a friend in a post or comment, or identify them in a photograph on social media. In text, you usually tag them by adding the @ symbol before their name. It's sometimes called an @ *mention* – the tagged friend will get a notification about the post or photo.

T&Cs/Ts & Cs – *Terms and Conditions*. The T&Cs are written by the promoter and are what every entrant agrees to when they take part in a competition or prize draw. They should include important details about the promotion, including (but not limited to) the closing date, prize details and entry restrictions.

Text message – Short messages sent between phones. For prize promotions in the UK, entrants usually have to text a keyword plus their name to a five-digit *short code*.

Third party – A *third party* entry is one that has been completed on behalf of the entrant by somebody else.

Tiebreaker – a question or challenge to decide the winner of a competition.

Timeline – the list of posts on a user's profile page on Instagram, Facebook or Twitter. On Facebook, this used to be called a *wall*.

Tweet – A message sent via *Twitter*.

Tweetdeck – A desktop or web-based app to manage Twitter. *Tweetdeck* offers multiple column feeds plus the ability to schedule tweets.

Twitter – An online social networking service where users send and read short messages (140 characters or less) called *tweets*.

UGC – *User Generated Content*. This refers to content created by consumers and available on websites or social media – it could be competition entries such as photos, videos, recipes or tiebreaker entries, which are shared on an app, social media or website by a promoter.

URL – A *Uniform Resource Locator* is the unique address for a file that is accessible on the internet (usually a website!).

URN – *Unique Reference Number*, sometimes called a *unique* code or *PIN* code. Usually a mixture of numbers and letters, and found on a promotional *instant win* product.

Viral – When something goes *viral*, word quickly spreads amongst friends on social media.

WEM – A *Winning Email* (notification of a win sent via email).

Winning moment – Some instant win promotions offer a prize to the first entrant to enter after (or during) a *winning moment*. This is a second, or a fraction of a second.

WOL – *Words or Less*. Australian term for slogan competition, eg. *25WOL*.

Woobox – An app used to run sweepstakes and competitions, usually requiring Facebook log in.

WTC – *Winning Telephone Call*. This will often be from a private or witheld number.

Resources

UK Competition websites & forums

www.theprizefinder.com

www.compersnews.com

http://forums.loquax.co.uk/forumdisplay.php?f=7

http://forums.moneysavingexpert.com/forumdisplay.php?f=72

www.hotukdeals.com/all/competitions/new

US Competition websites & forums

contests.about.com

www.online-sweepstakes.com

www.sweetiessweeps.com

www.contestgirl.com

Canadian Competition websites & forums

www.contestqueen.com

www.contestcanada.com

www.redflagdeals.com

Australian Competition websites & forums

www.competitions.com.au

www.aussiecontests.com

www.competitionguide.com.au

About the author

Di Coke is a Brighton-based blogger and author, and is passionate about well organised and fun competitions and prize draws. With £250,000 of prizes under her belt, Di is proud to be one of the UK's most prolific 'compers', and started her blog at **SuperLucky. Me** in 2009 to share advice on how to find and win consumer competitions.

As well as helping people to win their dream prize, Di consults with brands and agencies to ensure their prize promotions are creative, legal and a success.

Di has published two books, *'Blog Giveaways: how to run successful competitions, contests and prize draws on your blog'* and *'SuperLucky Secrets: 100 tips for winning competitions, contests and sweepstakes'*, and writes a monthly column for Compers News magazine. Di has appeared on BBC Breakfast, ITV Weekend and The Morning Show, and hosted sessions on running prize promotions at major UK blogging events Cybher, BritMums Live and Blogstock.

Get in touch with Di at **www.superlucky.me**, by email at **di@ superlucky.me**, or tweet to **@superluckydi**.

Where to find me

Blog – **http://superlucky.me**

Email – **di@superlucky.me**

Facebook profile – **www.facebook.com/dicoke**

Facebook page – **www.facebook.com/superlucky.co.uk**

Twitter – **@superluckydi**

Instagram – **@superluckydi**

Pinterest – **www.pinterest.com/dicoke**

YouTube – **www.youtube.com/superluckydi**

Join my mailing lists

If you'd like to receive my regular newsletter for compers, sign up at **superlucky.me/newsletter**.

If you'd like to join my mailing list for bloggers and promoters, sign up at **superlucky.me/checklist**.

Join my Facebook groups

- **Lucky Learners**: make friends with other compers, and get support and advice on your new hobby.

- **Competition Winners**: search for your missed competition wins *(UK only)*.

- **Facebook Competitions**: find and share Facebook competitions *(UK only, members must already be in the Lucky Learners group)*.

About SuperLucky.Me

My blog at **www.superlucky.me** is split into several sections – there's also a *Search this website* box for you to easily find the content you need. I post several times a week, so be sure to visit regularly to find out what's happening in the world of comping!

Get Started > my beginner's guide to comping.

Competitions > find UK blog giveaways, daily draws and instant wins here, plus the latest creative comps and my own exclusive giveaways.

For Promoters > advice for companies and bloggers on running fair and fun promotions.

Inspiration > my prize reports and diary, plus read all about successful compers in my *#SuperLuckyStories* and *Meet the Compers* series.

Winning tips > Advice on every aspect of comping.

"Di is a respected member of the comping community. As well as openly sharing her many years of comping experience, she works tirelessly behind the scenes trying to ensure competitions are run fairly and above board, naming and shaming unscrupulous companies that are not doing so. Di is a great source of comping information and is keen to share her valuable knowledge: from encouraging us to source low entry creative comps to explaining how to make entries stand out from the crowd. Her enthusiasm knows no bounds, it's addictive and motivates everyone around to start entering competitions!" – Julie Ellis

---

Index

Printed in Great Britain
by Amazon.co.uk, Ltd.,
Marston Gate.